Advance Praise for *Going Online with Protocols*

"Structures to make sure learners meet each other, have clear goals and norms, and share voices equally are absent in so many online courses and forums, where conversation threads are often random and unproductive. Thankfully, there is a remedy: Read this practical and astute book."

—**Ron Berger**, Chief Program Officer, Expeditionary Learning

"This book breathes new life into the struggle to create a rich, protected, and safe space for social learning and to help participants adjust to it. Eduplanet21 has already included some of the protocols in its instructional design. Thanks for all of the ideas!"

—**Jeff Colosimo**, CEO, Eduplanet21

"In this engaging and thoughtful book, the authors lay out tools and share a bounty of resources and experiences. Whether you are novice or experienced in using protocols or engaging in online learning, this book offers new learning and new adventures."

—**Frances Hensley**, Founding President, School Reform Initiative

"Talk about 21st-century skills! *Going Online with Protocols* shows us how technology extends the power of protocols to support the learning of real teachers and real students."

—**David Allen**, Assistant Professor of English Education, College of Staten Island, the City University of New York

"*Going Online with Protocols* is a powerful text that provides educators with the necessary tools to guide students through meaningful discussion in an online environment. The authors provide a great collection of practical tools to improve student success in online learning. No online educator should be without it!"

—**Suzanne M. Ehrlich**, Director and Assistant Professor, Signed Language Interpreting program, University of Cincinnati

D0833125

Going Online
with **Protocols**

Going Online
with **Protocols**

New Tools for Teaching and Learning

Joseph P. McDonald
Janet Mannheimer Zydney
Alan Dichter
Elizabeth C. McDonald

Teachers College
Columbia University
New York and London

Published by Teachers College Press, 1234 Amsterdam Avenue, New York, NY 10027

Library of Congress Cataloging-in-Publication Data

Going online with protocols : new tools for teaching and learning /
    Joseph P. McDonald ... [et al.].
        p. cm.
    Includes bibliographical references and index.
    ISBN 978-0-8077-5357-6 (pbk. : alk. paper)
        1. Web-based instruction. 2. Computer network protocols. I. McDonald, Joseph P.
    LB1044.87.G65 2012
    371.33'44678—dc23   2012023554

ISBN 978-0-8077-5357-6 (paperback)

Printed on acid-free paper
Manufactured in the United States of America

19   18   17   16   15   14   13   12   8   7   6   5   4   3   2   1

For Mike, Bradley, Vivian, Ben, Jacob,
and adventurous teachers everywhere

Contents

Acknowledgments

We begin by thanking our extraordinary colleagues at the University of Cincinnati, at New York University, at the Portland Public Schools, and elsewhere who have generously allowed us to draw upon their work. We were inspired by online and protocol adventurers Ron Berger, Tina Blythe, Cliff Cohen, Aimee deNoyelles, Funda Ergulec, Steve Goodman, Glynda Hull, Paul Jones, Fred Kaiser, Alyson Mike, Pam Rankey, Rosa Pietanza, Donna Schnupp, Steve Seidel, Kay Kyeong-Ju Seo, and Steven Strull. We are grateful for the numerous others who originated protocols that we have adapted—especially Patricia Averette, Daniel Baron, Patricia Carini, Kathy Juarez, Steve Seidel, Gene Thompson-Grove, and the late great Nancy Mohr. Their collective work (with that of many others) has spawned a new pedagogy that we describe in this book. A special thanks to colleagues who joined our Jumping into the Future contest by contributing provocative new protocols (see Chapter 7): David Allen, Anne Burgunder, and Miriam Raider-Roth.

We also thank a group of institutions whose work we describe here; they include the Johns Hopkins University, the Kidnet Project and Space2cre8, New Teacher Center, the School Reform Initiative, the Steinhardt School at New York University, the University of Cincinnati, and the University of Michigan.

Finally, we thank our families, who put up with our many hours of writing, Skyping, and ignoring them (temporarily), including Michael J. and Bradley Zydney Mannheimer, Vivian Orlen, Ben and Jacob Roter, and Harry (the dog) who escaped to Idaho early in the history of this book but eventually learned to embrace our purpose.

Finally, thanks to our adventurous and patient editors at Teachers College Press.

CHAPTER 1

Introduction

This book is about new tools for teaching and learning in the 21st century. It was written for everyone interested in teaching. It also contains an explicit invitation for two sets of educational adventurers to meet up. The first is experienced with what are called *protocols*, by virtue of their work in school reform and curriculum reform at all levels. The second is experienced in online teaching, by virtue of their use of new and emerging technologies (or for other reasons we explain below). Our invitation to both of these groups is based on the premise that they can benefit from getting to know each other and, moreover, that they really *need* to meet. It is also based on our sense that all the rest of us can learn a lot from the work they may end up doing together.

The protocol adventurers are in the process of elaborating a pedagogy that is very useful for online environments—one that online teachers seem hungry for. Meanwhile, the online adventurers are experienced in a phenomenon likely to sweep through all of education over the next decade. Other teachers will need the guidance of their experience, likely, sooner than they think.

Currently, what we'll call protocol teachers and online teachers inhabit different worlds and, consequently, have cultural barriers to overcome in the collaboration we propose. Indeed, as we discuss below, even the word *protocol* means different things within their respective worlds, and the difference requires understanding and negotiation. So it often happens when one crosses borders: The familiar becomes strange and vice versa. However, there are few better ways to gain new insight into old matters than by crossing borders.

PROTOCOLS: THREE SEMINAL EXAMPLES

As we use the term here, *protocols* were first developed by school reformers beginning in the 1990s, building on a few earlier prototypes. They share not only the name but certain features of the protocols long associated with experimental science, computer science, social science, medicine, and diplomacy. Like these others, the protocols that concern us in this book involve prearranged constraints designed to sharpen communication, enhance collective thinking, and build knowledge. For example, a seminal school reform protocol called the Tuning Protocol is among the most constraining of protocols. It constrains *who* speaks *when*, for *how long, about what,* and *with what focus.* So the protocol allots, say, 10 minutes to one teacher's uninterrupted presentation to his colleagues of a proposal to revamp the math curriculum. This is followed by, say, 10 minutes more for the colleagues to *tune* it. They do this by providing feedback (also in an uninterrupted fashion—no questions or conversation permitted) in the form of separate *warm* comments and *cool* comments. The first category of comments focuses on merits and strengths, and the second, on drawbacks and shortcomings. The presenting teacher listens to both but does not respond. The facilitator of a Tuning Protocol typically ensures that the warm and cool feedback stays balanced, and may even cut off a reviewer in mid-sentence if he or she starts out warm and then turns cool within the same comment. "Let warm and cool stand on their own," the facilitator may explain. "They both deserve attention." The protocol ends with a chance (uninterrupted) for the presenter to reflect on the feedback and to respond to it. Typically, presenters reserve some parts of the feedback for further thought and later response (maybe the next draft via email), and the facilitator reminds everyone that the tuning is part of a longer process, not the concluding step. Typically too, a presenter expresses gratitude to the participants for seriously considering his or her ideas, for listening carefully, and for offering deep and honest feedback. And sometimes the tuners themselves express gratitude for having been listened to (a rare phenomenon in much human discourse) and for having been pressed to think in both warm and cool terms (also rare). These are the payoffs for which both parties tolerate all those constraints.

While the Tuning Protocol forces balanced critique, other protocols, like the Consultancy protocol, force low-inference description, balanced at points by speculation. In the process, they hone new skills of perception, thinking, and discussion. The Consultancy protocol in particular expands participants' question-posing skills. Presenters learn to ask what are called *focusing questions* about a dilemma or problem from their practice—one they bring to a group of colleagues or strangers who serve as their consultants. These aim to capture succinctly what the presenters hope to learn from the consultants. For their part, the consultants learn to ask *clarifying questions* meant to ferret out the elements of what is, to them, a novel situation, but without imposing premature interpretive frames or pressing for deeper analysis. For example, the consultants may ask the presenter about details left out of the presentation that may possibly be important (e.g., how many students he or she teaches, how the students are grouped, how the groups are assessed, etc.). By definition, these are easy questions for the presenter to answer because they are factual from his or her perspective. At the same time, they require discipline on the consultant's part—indeed the discipline *of* a consultant—to get all the facts in a way that does not rush to judgment. Consultants also learn to ask what are called *probing questions*, and presenters learn how to answer them. These questions extend the discipline of the protocol beyond fact gathering into genuine client-centered consulting. Probing questions are designed to push the presenter's thinking deeper without pushing a particular solution to the problem or dilemma. To guide consultants in their construction of probing questions, David Allen and Tina Blythe (2004) offer several tips in the form of what are really probing questions themselves: Do I have a right answer in mind? (If so, the question is *not* a probing question); Is my question relevant to the presenter's focusing question? (If not, I'm not consulting effectively); and Does my question encourage the presenter to take a risk without making him or her feel threatened or accused? (If it doesn't gently support risk taking, then it's not worth the time it takes to ask and answer).

Similarly, participants in a Collaborative Assessment Conference—another seminal protocol, and our third example—learn to describe student work in a way that keeps all but low inference at bay. For example, the facilitator might begin, "What do you *see* in this child's drawing?" and discourage responses like "self-confidence" or "immaturity" while welcoming responses like "thick lines" and "the color blue." The point is to begin an analysis in the most concrete and objective way, as a necessary prelude to seeing beyond what one expects to see. Collaborative Assessment Conference participants also learn to ask deep questions about student work—ones that frequently stimulate deeper insights into teaching. Finally, participants learn to speculate about what a particular student is working on—perhaps the most useful of the protocol's disciplines. In the process, they may discover, for example, that the student is not just working on the teacher's assignment but on an implicit agenda of his or her own construction—and one that may or may not be consonant with the teacher's agenda.[1]

PROTOCOL ADVENTURE

In this book, we refer to more than 40 protocols in ways that we hope will encourage you to try them out. To support you in this trying out, we will either spell out all the steps of the protocol (as in Chapters 4, 5, 6, and 7), or point you to other print and online resources that provide the steps (as we have with respect to the three protocols described above). And you can follow our references to find hundreds of other protocols that implicitly teach other disciplined orientations toward doing things like making presentations, exploring texts of various types, and giving and getting advice.

Although many protocols are less tightly controlled than the Tuning Protocol, the Consultancy, and Collaborative Assessment Conference, all feel nonetheless artificial to some extent. Consequently, participants new to protocols sometimes ask, "Why can't we *just talk*?" But their facilitators typically urge them instead to tolerate awhile their discomfort. "It's like a game," they may say, echoing Douglas Thomas and John Seely Brown (2011), who write that the boundaries of a game are not just constraints but also potential catalysts for innovation. This is the allure of both games and protocols, and also, as we say, their payoff. "Besides," a facilitator might add, "*Just talking* often leads to some of us talking too much and others talking too little." Moreover, *just talking* can lead to talk full of obfuscation and indirection. By contrast, protocols tend to move things along—simply because they often *structure in* movement. For example, the three protocols mentioned above each conclude with the presenter's reflections on possible next steps toward revising a proposal, resolving a dilemma, or working with a particular student. Similarly, the Instructional Rounds in Education protocol ends with a step called Next Level of Work, in which participants take what they've learned from observing instruction within a school they are visiting, and from a collaborative analysis of their observation data, to a consideration of what concrete steps the school might take to move its instruction to a "next level"[2] With some protocols, the next level may involve richer and more complex assessment. For example, the protocol called What Comes Up? forces everyone around a table to answer the title question with regard to some input—often a piece of student work—What comes up for you when you read this poem written this morning by a third grader? What comes up for you when you see this video clip of one of our student interns teaching? In a game-like way, the protocol forbids any repeat comments. What comes up for one respondent must be different from what came up for a previous respondent, though the facilitator advises that no comment is too small, that everything is worth noticing. Thus the protocol presses participants to explore the input deeply and broadly, to listen intently to each other (if only so as not to repeat), and to stretch the collective response.[3]

We have lots more to say about protocols in Chapter 2—about their origin, their key characteristics, and the values that underlie them. Three of the four authors of this book (Joe, Alan, and Beth) are also authors of a book called *The Power of Protocols: An Educator's Guide to Better Practice* (McDonald, Mohr, Dichter, & McDonald, 2007). In that book, they and their coauthor, the late Nancy Mohr, emphasize the traditional use of school reform protocols for planning, accessing external expertise, reviewing data, and looking together at student work. In this book, by contrast, we emphasize the derivative use of protocols for teaching. As it turns out, many educators who become acquainted with protocols as part of working together and learning together with colleagues end up keeping the protocols in mind as they plan their own teaching. These are the protocol adventurers we especially highlight in this book. They are the ones, for example, who teach even young children how to use the Tuning Protocol for peer editing or to give each other warm and cool feedback after presentations. Or they teach small groups of older students how to use the Consultancy to give each other useful feedback on projects or internships that are under way.

ONLINE ADVENTURE

The second set of educational adventurers whom we highlight in this book are online teachers, including those who teach in what are called *blended settings*—partly online and partly face-to-face.[4] Their adventurousness is sometimes associated with a sense that social media tools—often called Web 2.0 tools—have an inherent power to transform education in massive and beneficial ways.[5] Some online teachers really want to be part of this action (Chen, 2010; Thomas & Brown, 2011). But market forces as well as vision play a role too (Palloff & Pratt, 2011). Thus increasing numbers of online teachers today have been swept up in the efforts of many institutions of higher education to expand their customer base through online coursework. Both the teachers and their students may be victimized, as Jason Snart (2010) suggests, by a pernicious idea that online teaching is easier and cheaper than conventional face-to-face teaching.

In *Education Nation*, Milton Chen (2010) traces what we now call online teaching to mid-19th-century England. That's where Sir Isaac Pitman (arguably the Steve Jobs of his day for having invented shorthand) also had the idea of using the newly launched "Penny Post" mail service to institute mass correspondence courses. From then until now, people everywhere have used "distance education" to meet work-focused and leisure-focused educational needs and aspirations. Do you want to repair engines, grow roses, paint landscapes, cook paella? If so, someone has a webinar, blog, or YouTube video for you. Gradually too, educators at nearly every level have learned to use these devices for more systemic educational purposes—that is, to advance their students' qualifications for diplomas and degrees, and to train them for professions. In this book, we are principally concerned with this latter kind of teaching. It typically happens in elementary schools, secondary schools, and what are called institutions of higher education in the United States.

The most active educational sector in online teaching today is higher education. The 2011 report of the Sloan Consortium, which has tracked the rise of online teaching in U.S. higher education over nearly a decade, reports that about 31% of higher education students now take at least one course online—or 6.1 million students in the fall of 2010, a 10% increase over the previous year (Allen & Seaman, 2011). For-profit higher education institutions make up a disproportionately large part of this growing sector, but large, public higher education institutions remain the real online leaders. The Sloane data suggest that the latter lead in enthusiasm for the enterprise, as almost 80% of these institutions report that online education is a vital component of their long-term strategy (Allen & Seaman, 2011). Online learning environments, and sometimes blended learning environments, enable higher education institutions to reach numerous customers they otherwise could not reach—a major attraction for public institutions seeking to justify public expenditures. These audiences include students who live far from the campus and cannot take up residence on or near it, as well as students living anywhere in the state who are unable to take face-to-face courses because of work schedules, family obligations, disabilities, or other reasons. Of course, they also include out-of-state students who pay higher tuitions, including foreign students who, for many reasons, cannot easily take up residence in the United States.

Meanwhile, online learning environments can stretch the boundaries of what *can be* learned, because they expand the boundaries of the learning experience. For example, a foreign-language teacher can enable his or her students to converse with people who speak the target language even if they live on the other side of the world. A history teacher can arrange for students to interview a historian whose book they are reading or to read documents that in the recent past would have required extraordinary travel and other arrangements. A science teacher can engage students around the world in the collection of data relative to an inquiry. A women's studies teacher can have her or his students take on avatars in a 3-D multiuser virtual environment in order to experience living as a person of another gender. And a pre-med teacher can invite students to travel as blood cells through a virtual human heart. Note that some of these examples of online learning do not necessarily involve distance learning. In this book we also sometimes use the terms *online teaching* and *blended teaching* to refer to situations in which teacher and learners occupy contiguous space but substantially supplement face-to-face learning with tasks completed alone and together online.

Online education is growing fast today within K–12 education too, though online education remains a tiny slice of a gigantic enterprise and also faces special challenges. For the moment, its importance lies less in its scale and more in its adaptation (sometimes controversial) to what McDonald, Klein, and Riordan (2009) call changes in the constitution of American schooling (i.e., the creation of new kinds of institutions, governance systems, and formats). For example, the for-profit corporation K12, an industry leader with a half-billion dollars of revenue in 2011, currently manages the instruction of more than 82,000 students in statewide virtual or blended public schools in 27 states (K12, 2011).[6]

Elementary or secondary students who study online include those who have chosen, for various reasons and for various stretches, to attend an online public school (perhaps a charter school) or an online private one. Other online learners may be homeschooled students whose parents or guardians are supported by online instructional services; homebound students whose school districts purchase online services for them; or students attending what online educators call "brick and mortar schools," where they avail themselves of supplemental online instruction arranged by the schools. Such schools may, for example, offer online a hard-to-staff foreign-language or technical course or a low-demand advanced placement course. Increasingly, these schools not only include isolated rural ones (an old online customer), but also urban ones. In addition to offering whole courses online, some of these schools use online instructional services to offer remediation in particular subjects or what is sometimes called credit recovery (bringing up a failing grade with targeted learning). Finally, online-engaged schools today may include big suburban high schools—the kind that Powell, Farrar, and Cohen (1985) famously called "shopping-mall high schools"—whose students and families, today, as always and for better or worse, demand more curricular variety, and whose faculties have (more or less skillfully) figured out how to operate within a blended environment.

HOW THIS BOOK IS ORGANIZED

As we said above, this book is for everybody interested in teaching, but also invites protocol teachers and online teachers to meet up and collaborate in the interest of improving teaching generally. This chapter is the invitation itself. The next two chapters provide deeper background briefings. Chapter 2 says, "Let me tell you more about protocol-based teaching and learning." Then, Chapter 3 says, "Let me tell you more about online teaching and learning." Readers from both worlds will find points of interest in both chapters, however, because both are constructed to offer fresh perspectives on the familiar and the unfamiliar.

The practical heart of the book is all the rest—Chapters 4 through 7. Chapter 4 describes in detail online protocols helpful in beginning a course or other learning experience—getting students to know one another, enabling them to organize themselves into small working groups and orienting them to whatever content is being taught. We call these *protocols for starting up*. Chapter 5 describes in detail protocols for delving in—namely, those that help students interact deeply with each other and the content. And Chapter 6 describes in detail what we call protocols for finishing up, which help teachers conclude a learning experience, enabling students, for example, to get final feedback on their work or to reflect on the major themes of what they have learned. Finally, Chapter 7 describes in detail a few ambitious online protocols still in a state of development.

We have written all these chapters in the style of *The Power of Protocols*—that is, with purposes, details, steps, and suggested variations of the protocols spelled out in turn. We mean these directions to invite collaboration rather than replication, however. Indeed, if *Going Online with Protocols* were itself a blended teaching and learning environment instead of just a book, these chapters would be *wikis*. For those readers for whom a definition of *wiki* may not quickly spring to mind, we offer Jason Snart's (2010) succinct one: "A wiki is a Web site that can be quickly, or at least easily accessed, edited, and expanded by a collaborative group of users" (p. 120). Many of you likely know Wikipedia—the wiki-based online encyclopedia—and may be familiar with the fact that readers of its entries can change those entries. Because wikis are web-based, they can also incorporate audio, video, and links to other levels of text and to other websites. Alas, this book is just a book, whose only hypertext powers come from the usual sources: images, endnotes, and references. But we ask you to read our protocol descriptions *as if* they were wikis. In other words, change entries by engaging in your own adventures as you read about ours and those of the colleagues we cite. Call on *your* colleagues to join you as we've called on ours, or link up with other teachers online. Start a Facebook group. Play, chat.[7] In the process, draw on our downloadable protocols at www.tcpress.com.

Now, if you are brand new to online teaching and learning, and prefer a non–Web 2.0 analogy for what we are suggesting, then think *cookbook*. Nobody ever reads *through* a cookbook—as if, for example, the salad section were a non-fiction chapter. Nor should you do that with our Chapters 4, 5, 6, and 7. Browse them instead, then dive in and try something. Spill olive oil on the pages, so to speak. That is, figure out how to engage physically with these protocols. Do this somehow—actually or virtually—in the company of others. Start a kind of cookbook club online, or become a social bookmarker with regard to teaching online with protocols.[8]

ORIGINS OF THE BOOK

You already know that three of the authors of this book wrote another book about protocols first published nearly a decade ago, though newly available in a third edition. While working on that book, these three authors ran into a young doctoral student of educational technology at New York University (NYU) named Janet Mannheimer Zydney. Spurred on by Beth McDonald and Nancy Mohr, Janet helped create and piloted a protocol as part of a research project she was then conducting. Called the Shadow Protocol, it is featured in all editions of *The Power of Protocols*, and is widely used today by groups of teachers aiming to supplement available data on students whom the teachers find puzzling. By means of the Shadow Protocol, these teachers gain up-close but low-inference accounts of how these students actually work and learn on a typical school day, and also how they respond to the intellectual challenges they encounter within and between classes. An important feature of the protocol is that the students themselves contribute substantially to the new data, and thus help themselves to solve the puzzlement they inspired. In other words, the protocol offers them a sense of agency at a problematic juncture in their education. After all, being a puzzle to your teachers is usually not a good thing for your learning. When Janet designed the protocol, this teaching function was not uppermost in her mind. It seems to us now, however, emblematic of the phenomenon we explore here (in Chapter 2), whereby a protocol originally designed to be a tool for teachers' learning becomes a teaching method too.

After getting her PhD in educational technology, Janet joined the faculty of the University of Cincinnati, where she teaches mostly in blended formats. She is, in short, a bona fide technologist, a bona fide protocol teacher, and an online teacher. One day, on a visit to New York, she told Joe and Beth that she had also become a protocol teacher *online*. This happened, she said, when she encountered in her online teaching many of the same challenges that she knew protocols addressed in face-to-face teaching (e.g., how to keep students engaged, how to help them appreciate and value diverse ideas, how to encourage quiet students to add their voices to the conversation, how to help everyone listen more purposefully, etc.). Indeed, by the time of that lunch, she had already teamed up with some colleagues to create a professional learning community focused on adapting protocols to online settings. Might the authors of *The Power of Protocols*, Janet asked, be interested in writing a new book to explore the application of protocols in online teaching, drawing on the work of her Cincinnati colleagues? As it turned out, Joe, Beth, and Alan had already been talking about a sequel to the earlier book—one exploring the emergence of a protocol pedagogy, as well as professional learning communities working to explore and expand that pedagogy.[9] They eagerly embraced Janet's idea and asked her to join them in the writing.

In time, the core image of this book emerged from our conversations, namely the image of adventurers meeting up to plan further adventures. In the process, we had our own small adventures—ones we describe below for the sake of readers who may at this point be worried that the adventures we are suggesting are only for highly experienced adventurers and that people like us may be immune from the techno-gaffes and glitches that often plague those readers.

Our first virtual meeting as a team to discuss this book was arranged by Janet on a platform the other authors had never used before, namely Adobe Connect Web conference. Janet was in Cincinnati, where she teaches; Alan, in Portland, Oregon, where he lives; and Beth and Joe, in New

York City, with Joe at home and Beth at her NYU office. Janet set up the call, and Alan signed on first. They could see that they were both online but could neither see nor hear each other. However, they could communicate through the chat feature of the conferencing site.[10] While Alan worked on his audio issues, Janet got a phone call from Joe, who was not sure how to get started. He had meant to read Janet's directions earlier, but forgot. Soon Beth logged on. Alan had, in the meantime, resolved his audio issues, so now he and Janet could hear Beth. However, Beth could not hear Janet and Alan. Janet then called Beth on her cell phone and figured out that her sound was muted, but Beth still could not see or be seen because she did not have a built-in camera on her computer. Finally, Joe logged on. He did have a portable video mount for his laptop, but couldn't find the camera icon to activate it. Still, everyone could at least hear one another. Unfortunately, though, not everyone had yet purchased headsets (despite Janet's urging), so the *hearing* involved lots of echoes—amid which genuine discussion proved elusive.

Still, we were determined not to let these technology glitches befuddle us—the theme of this little story. Sure, some of us did privately think at the moment, "I'm going to write a book about online teaching, and I can't even pull *this* off?" But we laughed at our predicament instead, and promised (amid all the echoes) to include this story in our opening chapter, as if to say, "Expect this and learn to tolerate and work through this." And we plodded on—switching to voice conferencing through Skype.[11] Sadly, however, this brought its own set of problems. First, Alan couldn't remember his Skype username, though he gave Janet a couple of options and she was able to find him. Then Joe called Janet on her cell phone to say that he had forgotten his Skype password. True, he had stored the password on his Blackberry, but the Blackberry had been charging all night by mistake with the GPS charger, and now lacked juice. Joe thus had to reset his password, which took several minutes. Finally, he was able to log on to Skype but, for some reason, proved unable to join the call under way. Janet tried a couple of times, but couldn't quickly figure out a way to add him. To save time, she decided to restart the conference call. This time, all four of us got to talk together for exactly 3 minutes—in the end, the most successful connection of the entire hour. Then Beth got dropped. The other three authors carried on for 5 minutes more, but then decided to end our first book meeting. As you see, however, we had already laid the basis for a portion of Chapter 1.

Shortly afterward, Joe Skyped Beth at her office to fill her in on what she had missed from the last 5 minutes of the call but, again, she got dropped.

However, she quickly Skyped back, and she and Joe remained well connected thereafter. In the course of their conversation, Joe invited their dog
Harry to get online too and greet his mother. But Harry freaked out and
promptly headed for his hiding place under the bed—a place Joe and Beth
call his own private Idaho.[12] It's a place where many humans also sometimes scurry to in the face of connectivity problems like these. We believe
that they do so mostly because they think that others do not experience
the same problems. In fact, in these still early years of Web 2.0, everybody
does. Moreover, everybody—of any age— can acquire the patience to work
through such problems and get started with online learning.

CHAPTER 2

Protocol-Based Teaching and Learning

Everyone at NYU who studies to be a teacher or counselor takes a one-credit course called "The Social Responsibilities of Educators," which meets a long list of state requirements for licensure. These include, for example, knowledge of the regulations on child abuse; the responsibilities of educators with regard to substance abuse prevention, domestic violence prevention, and bullying; and awareness of safety precautions with regard to fire, child abduction, and HIV infection. These topics are important to educational practice, and vital from the perspective of education as a caring profession, but the original design of the course failed to engage students. The problem was not the licensure checklist, but the painfully piecemeal way the course addressed it: a lecture/discussion "covering" a particular topic—one a week for 15 weeks. The result was that the topics themselves—and crucially, too, the instructors' considerable knowledge and experience of them—were reduced to PowerPoint presentations, war stories, and desultory discussion. The instructors were experts—but in diverse respects. However, they never came into more than perfunctory contact with each other because they taught alone. In what turned out to be a forlorn effort to encourage student participation, the gigantic student enrollment in the course each year was broken into sections of about 30 students with a separate instructor for each section.

Advisors tended to tell students: "Just put up with the course. It's only an hour a week, it's required, and it's easy." That's a line that should provoke curriculum revision whenever it is uttered, and in this case did. But not before some students petitioned to take an outside vendor-sponsored online course. Some faculty checked out the proposed alternative and pronounced it dreadful: two hours of scrolling text plus a quiz. As Guralnick and Larson (2009) point out, this used to be the look of much online coursework—particularly workplace-related coursework. The faculty decided to deny the petition to substitute, but it also decided to redesign the course. The result prefigures a lot of what we discuss in this chapter.

As it happened, some of the faculty members involved in the redesign were what we call *protocol teachers*.[1] That is, they had gained experience in facilitating protocols within professional development settings, and had carried this experience into their teaching. Thus, part of their new design—now in its sixth year—resembles a professional conference, featuring protocol-guided panel discussions.

The first panel involves the same kind of experts who used to teach the old version of the course alone—health professionals, social workers, and educators. Now, however, they get to talk with each other, build on each other's expertise, and sometimes even disagree—all to the benefit of the students who get to hear them (though, as you will see, not right away). The teaching and learning is guided by the Panel Protocol, developed by Alan Dichter. Alan recalls developing it after suffering through one too many panel-based presentations where moderators promise enough time at the end for audience interaction, but never manage to wrest it from the panelists (McDonald et al., 2007). Thus the protocol flips the typical sequence of who talks first when experts and novices assemble. Here the students first wrestle with short cases the panelists have brought, and the panelists merely eavesdrop as they do. The students not only analyze the facets of their case but write the analyses on wall posters for others to see, along with their recommended action steps for resolving the case. The panelists review these posters (as students themselves do) in a protocol within a protocol called Gallery Walk.[2] When the panelists finally get to talk, they talk not only about what they had prepared to talk about, but also about what they've just overheard and reviewed—for example, questions they hadn't considered, misconceptions they sensed, information gaps they perceived, and so on.

A second panel in the conference portion of the course uses another protocol to give voice to those who are often *talked about* in educational conferences but seldom heard from—in this case, actual adolescents from New York's South Bronx and Lower East Side—sometimes as many as 20 of them.[3] The facilitator first prompts these middle- and high-school students to give the new teachers and counselors in the room their best advice on teaching and otherwise interacting with kids like them. The youth speak one after another in what protocol teachers call a go-round. "Be friendly, but don't try to be my friend," one might say. Others say, "Be strict." "Get to know me." "Respect me." They often talk too about the kind of environments they need to do their best learning and about their lives beyond school. Warmed up by this task (a first public-speaking engagement for most of them), each panelist then joins a table for intimate and always animated follow-up conversation.

Finally, the new version of the course has an online component—making it blended. Instead of scrolling text, however, students encounter prompts that guide inquiries into their own field settings, and today they also follow protocols in exploring a range of Web-based texts, including videos. Oddly, however, the protocols did not immediately follow the course in going online. It took the Social Responsibilities instructors (who include one of the authors of this book, Joe) years to figure out that protocols can work well online too. For example, though the online learners were a keystroke or two away from hundreds of rich and relevant online documents (including videos, blogs, articles, data tables, and policy regulations), they were generally instructed, in analyzing a case or answering a question about school violence or child abuse, to consult their (expensive) textbook and a circumscribed set of posted documents. Moreover, there was no use of social media—not even an online discussion group—to discuss what they were finding in their fieldwork. All this eventually turned around, however, when the course instructors suddenly realized that the way some online teachers think about protocols—as rules for posting (Gilbert & Dabbagh, 2005)—is not really all that different from the way they themselves think about protocols—as rules for collaborating. And it dawned on them that if students were invited to use social media of their own choice (for example, Facebook, Google Docs, or Google Talk) to make sense of what they were exploring, they would do so eagerly.[4]

WHERE DO PROTOCOLS COME FROM?

Protocols are artifacts of a broad idea about how to make organizations of all kinds more effective. The idea, simply put, is for the people of the organization to do their work in teams and within an environment that encourages (1) knowledge sharing, (2) joint responsibility for the quality of work output, and (3) an overall organizational culture of continuous improvement (Brown & Duguid, 2000; Deming, 1986; Senge, 1990; Wenger, 1998). In the late 1980s, this idea migrated from organizational theory, where it had focused mostly on the problem of rethinking 20th-century industrial design, to school reform. The result was what was sometimes called the school restructuring movement (Newmann, 1996).[5] Key contributors to the movement included Ted Sizer's Coalition of Essential Schools (home of the Tuning Protocol mentioned in Chapter 1) and Howard Gardner's Harvard Project Zero (home of the Collaborative Assessment Conference also mentioned in Chapter 1). The restructuring reformers held that certain features of American schooling—for example, isolated classroom teaching, hierarchical curriculum supervision, and the sorting of students into presumed levels of intellectual capacity—were as antiquated and ineffectual as assembly-line factories. The reformers proposed a different kind of schooling: more student-centered, intellectually ambitious, and team based. And to this end, they encouraged and supported small communities of reform-minded educators to engage in locally devised but nationally networked design experiments. The research of Fred Newmann (1996), Karen Seashore Louis and Helen Marks (1998), Linda Darling-Hammond and Gary Sykes (1999), and Milbrey McLaughlin and Joan Talbert (2001) found encouraging results in these efforts. For a brief time—before the explosive growth of accountability based more or less exclusively on state and federally mandated standardized testing—it seemed that the movement might be broadly influential (Darling-Hammond, Ancess, & Falk, 1995; McDonald, 1996). And in a sense, as we argue below, it was.

IMPACT ON PEDAGOGY

The restructuring reformers tended to be eclectic in their pedagogical preferences. Teaching strategies took a back seat in their view to the formulation of the right learning goals, attention to students as unique learners, and the creation of more collaborative teaching environments. However, the reformers recognized that schools and school communities would need lots of strategic assistance in achieving these front-seat goals, and they set out to help. David Allen's 1998 book *Assessing Student Learning: From Grading to Understanding* captures the spirit of this effort with accounts of a miscellany of development tools mostly designed to facilitate teachers' collaborative examination of student work. But "it often seems," Allen writes in the book's introduction, "that in looking at students' work samples, teachers are really looking—as in double exposure—at their own work" (p. 3).

Although Allen's book is often considered to be the first book about protocols, the word itself barely surfaces there. *Protocol* would only later become a general term applied to a broad array of tools designed to help educators educate themselves in "double exposure" accountability practice. Yet in a prospective way at least, Allen's book does identify the phenomenon we track in this chapter—namely the emergence of a *signature pedagogy* based on the use of such tools (more about this term below). Indeed, Howard Gardner's introduction to Allen's book is partly a call for such a pedagogy. He imagines one inspired by the likes of the Tuning Protocol and the Collaborative Assessment Conference—or more specifically by the teacher learning communities that invented these protocols.[6] These communities, Gardner writes, encourage their participants "to put their own understandings at risk, to construct new practices, to try them out, to receive feedback from friendly critics and critical friends, and to try again." He adds, "It is intriguing to realize" that such work among teachers "bears a significant resemblance to the work that teachers are—and will be—asking students to do." He ends by calling for a pedagogy that targets genuine understanding rather than "the piling on of facts" (p. viii). This pedagogy, he adds, "will be driven by real problems, involve experimentation, revision, and reflection, and require "a comfortable surrounding where one can speak one's mind without feeling threatened and without threatening others" (p. ix).

As we suggested, the teacher learning communities that Gardner and Allen wrote about were overshadowed by a more policy-centered and sanctions-oriented accountability. Still, they proved influential—playing important roles, for example, in the development of a small-school and charter-school movement (Siskin, 2011; Wasley et al., 2000); in the spread of professional learning communities (PLCs) and "critical friends groups" (Curry, 2008; DuFour, DuFour, Eaker, & Many, 2010); and in efforts to attend in a meaningful way to the data that test-based accountability generates (Boudett, City, & Murnane, 2005; Talbert, 2011). Meanwhile, wherever teacher communities surfaced, protocols often followed. In the process, a reserve of expertise in the facilitation of protocols accumulated—a crucial factor in the emergence of a signature pedagogy based on protocols. Organizations like the National School Reform Faculty (http://www.nsrfharmony.org/), founded by the Annenberg Institute at Brown University, and later the School Reform Initiative (http://schoolreforminitiative.org), both supported by the Bay and Paul Foundation, tended to the cultivation and distribution of this expertise, as well as the archiving of protocols themselves. David Allen, again, this time writing with Tina Blythe (2004), played an important role in curating the archive and illuminating the practices of protocol facilitators. Their book, called *The Facilitator's Book of Questions,* implicitly insists that the effective use of protocols in professional learning is less about the tools themselves than about the craft and dispositions of the facilitators. This remains a widely shared idea among experienced protocol facilitators—and as protocols have migrated into teaching, it has tagged along. The result is that what we call protocol pedagogy is less tool-focused than its name may suggest.

Indeed, as it turns out, the research on teacher learning communities and protocols bears out the value of this broader emphasis. Studies of the impact of teacher learning communities have consistently shown benefits for students, though only when the communities focus explicitly on increasing student learning (Curry, 2008; Little, Gearhart, Curry, & Kafka, 2003; McLaughlin & Talbert, 2006; Phillips, 2003; Supovitz, 2002; Supovitz & Christman, 2003; Vescio, Ross, & Adams, 2008). By contrast, when not tethered to questions of whether and what students are learning, teacher learning communities may have only a superficial impact. For example, in their studies of the use of small teacher communities as a reform strategy in Philadelphia and Cincinnati, Jon Supovitz and Jolley Christman (2003) found that while teachers liked working together in collaborative teams, the teams not explicitly focused on instructional improvement had no measurable positive impact on student learning. By contrast, the Cincinnati teams that used an instructionally focused protocol called Standards in Practice (SIP) outperformed teams that did not use the protocol, and they also outperformed teachers who were not members of collaborative teams but happened to use the protocol under other circumstances (Holtzapple, 2001).[7]

Judith Warren Little and her colleagues (2003) report similar findings in their study of schools using the Tuning Protocol and the Collaborative Assessment Conference. "The value of looking at student work," they write, "resides in its potential for bringing *students* more consistently and explicitly into deliberations among teachers" (p. 192, emphasis in original). Reporting on their research, Little and her colleagues also provide crucial early glimpses of how effective protocol groups work—and thus (for our purposes) clues to the elements that might make up an effective protocol pedagogy. First, the authors note that livelier and more productive conversations about student work occurred when groups were flexible in their choice and use of protocols—when, for example, they adjusted time limitations to suit the conversation or, even, dispensed with certain protocol constraints in order to pursue a compelling question. Second, the authors found that "the most generative conversations" occurred where participants invited challenge. "More important than the tools," they write, was "a facilitator who sought to open up a question or persist with a difficult point, a presenter who invited feedback by being self-critical or disclosing problems openly, a participant who took the risk to broach a controversial topic" (p. 190).

SIGNATURE PEDAGOGY

As we use the term, a *signature pedagogy* is one of a number of more or less distinct (from each other) instructional systems. Each is a collaboratively devised and flexible cultural artifact that has arisen in response to various theories, particularly about how people learn, plus various content demands (for example, how to read rich texts, solve complex design problems, or teach writing), various contextual factors (for example, how schools and colleges are designed), and various values (concerning, for example, equity). Although signature pedagogies have somewhat indistinct boundaries, they are nonetheless broadly distinct from each other in deep and surface features. The deep features are animating values and core ideas concerning how people learn and what is most important to learn (for example, in writing or mathematics or civics); while the surface features are the characteristic behaviors of teachers who practice the pedagogy. They have taught these behaviors to each other over time and typically within particular contexts. They use the behaviors both to make their work more efficient, and to signal to their students that they know what they're doing. We call these behaviors *moves*, using the word as a sports commentator might, to signify an athlete's (or, in our case, a teacher's) craft and the practice that sustains it.

So protocol pedagogy differs first from the pervasive lecture-and-discussion pedagogy of higher education, and the lecture-and-discussion-plus-seatwork pedagogy of K–12. Protocol pedagogy also differs from other less practiced and similarly adventurous pedagogies like Socratic or seminar pedagogy, games pedagogy, case study pedagogy, service learning pedagogy, project-and-expedition pedagogy, workshop pedagogy, and Doug Lemov pedagogy (he a chronicler of what is sometimes called "no excuses charter school" pedagogy).[8] There are dozens of signature pedagogies in use throughout the U.S. educational system, though only a small number approach pervasiveness and all rise and fall in popularity over time.

We borrow the term *signature pedagogy* from Lee Shulman who coined it for a related but more limited purpose than ours—namely, to explain the prevalence of certain kinds of teaching in professional education. His 2005 *Daedalus* article describes signature pedagogies as deliberate strategies for shaping novices' thinking and performing in ways that are valued within their professions. For example, there is the "paper chase" pedagogy, pervasive in the first year of law school, whereby, as Shulman writes, "An authoritative and often authoritarian instructor" engages a large group of students in the intricacies of a complex appellate case by asking a series of pressing questions focused on one student at a time (Shulman, 2005, p. 52). The students speak rarely to each other, just to the instructor, as, later in their careers, some of them may speak to an appellate judge. And there is the clinical rounds pedagogy, pervasive at a certain point in the education of physicians, whereby, a senior physician focuses a group of interns on a particular patient at bedside and presses the interns to ask the patient questions and determine symptoms through other means. Out of the patient's earshot, he or she asks his or her own pointed questions of the interns, pushing for alternative interpretations of the symptoms and narrowing toward a diagnosis and treatment plan. A gentler version of this pedagogy has also recently migrated into teacher education and the education of school leaders (City, Elmore, Fiarman, & Teitel, 2009; Del Prete, 2010)

The great value of signature pedagogies of any kind, as Shulman (2005) points out, is that they routinize teaching and learning—even teaching and learning difficult things. "Once [these signature pedagogies] are learned and internalized," he writes, "we don't have to think about them; we can think with them" (p. 56). And the predictability of a signature pedagogy can be reassuring to a student who has some reason (for example, a history of having been taught by inexperienced and ineffective teachers) for wondering whether the teacher is really prepared to deliver something of value. For their part, teachers who have mastered a signature pedagogy can reduce substantially the burden of preparing for every teaching encounter and, perhaps, spend more of their energy thinking about the content and the students.

There is, however, a downside to these efficiencies, as Shulman also acknowledges. Signature pedagogies exclude as much as they include, lend themselves better to certain kinds of learning than to other kinds, and may therefore distort comprehensive understanding. Moreover, they can lead to teaching rigidity—particularly, we would add, in circumstances of great learner diversity (urban schools and online environments come to mind). In the end, Shulman seems to advocate a balanced portfolio of pedagogies, and we heartily agree. Although we spend most of this chapter describing a signature pedagogy based on protocols, and though we think of protocol pedagogy as particularly well suited to online learning environments, we do not advocate incessant use of it there or anywhere else. And we would say the same about every other signature pedagogy. Indeed, Shulman calls for practitioners of various pedagogies to examine what the others know and can do. With this we also agree. He asks, for example, what laboratory science teachers can learn from the studio pedagogy of architects and of mechanical engineers.

PROTOCOL PEDAGOGY

We begin this exploration of protocol pedagogy by exploring why and how a single simple protocol might migrate into teaching. We take the one called the Triad Protocol, which Lois Easton describes in her 2009 book *Protocols for Professional Learning* and associates with getting feedback on work in progress. The matter of purpose is, of course, crucial to migration. Certainly, getting feedback on work in progress is an important dimension of genuine learning in any area of knowledge. So we can imagine how a teacher who had gotten useful feedback from his or her participation in a Triad Protocol on, say, a lesson plan, might think about using the protocol to afford his or her students useful feedback on, say, their essays, art projects, or robotic constructions. Moreover, the Triad Protocol is highly flexible, and flexibility is crucial to adaptation. For example, it has a typical duration of 30 to 45 minutes, which can be easily accommodated within almost any teaching situation. As Easton points out too, a Triad can be used in a group of any size so long as the group can be divided into subgroups of three. And if a particular class is not cleanly divisible by three, then the teacher can join a remainder pair and turn it into a triad. Some protocols require too much oversight for the facilitator to participate, but the Triad is easy to launch and lends itself well to self-direction.

In the first step of the protocol, each group of three participants decides who will be named A, B, or C. During the three rounds of the protocol, each letter signifies a role to be played by the corresponding participant, as follows:

Round 1: *A* presents his or her work in progress. Meanwhile, *B* serves as discussant, building on the presentation with comments, questions, and suggestions. And *C* serves as observer, listening carefully, saying nothing, and taking notes. After *A* and *B* have talked, *C* summarizes and adds a concluding comment.

Round 2: Here, *B* presents, while *C* discusses, and *A* observes.
Round 3: *C* presents, *A* discusses, and *B* observes.

That's it—except for a little debriefing (always a good step in a proto-col), plus—in a teaching situation—anything the teacher might want to do to build on the experience. For example, the teacher might ask each triad to huddle for a minute and come up with just one special thing they want to share with the whole group about being a presenter, discussant, or observer. These contributions could be listed on chart paper or projected on an interactive whiteboard and saved for the next time the class uses the Triad Protocol.

As we suggest, a teacher who had been a participant in a Triad as part of a professional development experience might be drawn toward using the protocol in teaching too. However, it is important to note that some teachers would not—including some who had enjoyed the experience and learned from it. These may be teachers who have never prepared their students to work successfully in self-directed, small groups, and tend therefore not to think in such terms when planning lessons. They may be teachers who think of their jobs in terms of *delivering* content, rather than *engaging* students with content. And they may be ones who do not value the learn-ing goals of this protocol (beyond getting feedback). By our count, these goals include learning to present effectively to peers, learning to listen care-fully to peer presentations, learning to initiate and steer effective discus-sions, learning to observe others' interactions and record them faithfully and insightfully, learning to summarize and conclude a conversation, and learning to risk practicing the above list of challenging behaviors before peers (and likely stumbling in the process). We ourselves think that these are hugely important 21st-century learning goals.

Teachers who would be drawn to trying out the Triad Protocol with their students—and who have done so—are not motivated just by the adaptability of it to classroom contexts, but by the fit of the protocol with their pedagogical values. They like its deep features.

DEEP FEATURES OF PROTOCOL PEDAGOGY

Arguably, one could highlight a greater number of deep features of pro-tocol facilitation and thus of protocol pedagogy, but we restrict ourselves here to four that we think have special resonance for the online teaching environment. And we explain this resonance along the way.

Pressing for Participation

The first deep feature is an exceptional emphasis on participation. "The special province of protocols," say David Allen and Tina Blythe in their 2004 book about facilitating protocols, "is in creating a space in which all participants, by virtue of their experience—no matter what that experience—can make important contributions to the conversation and, consequently, to the group's learning" (p. 28). Of course, most signature pedagogies prize what is often called classroom participation. For example, the chalk-and-talk high school teacher may provide a grade for it; the Lemov teacher and the Paper Chase teacher and the seminar teacher often "cold call" to obtain it. In protocols, however, the insistence is structured in—by means, for example, of "go-rounds," where everyone must speak in turn and find something new to say, or, as in the Triad Protocol, by forcing all to participate continuously and simultaneously by automatically distributing and redistributing roles. What happens in the process is that a joint responsibility emerges for ensuring participation. Everyone plays a role: no lurking, no silent voices. But no cold calls, no squirming. This is one of the ways that protocols are said to balance attention to the learning of individuals with attention to the learning of the group (Allen & Blythe, 2004).

This unusually strong and also unusually *distributed* attention to participation has a basis in research on learning. Echoing contemporary theorists in the learning sciences, D. R. Garrison and Terry Anderson (2003) write that every educational experience necessarily has both a personal and a social dimension. The purpose of the first is to construct new understanding in the learner's own experience, and the purpose of the second is "to refine and confirm this understanding collaboratively within a community of learners" (p. 13). Here is how we put it in *The Power of Protocols*:

> Learning is social. We inevitably learn through and with others, even though what is finally understood is our own mental construction (Bransford, Brown, & Cocking, 2000). In insisting that educators [or, from the perspective of this chapter, students] learning together get to know each other first, the facilitator is not just encouraging cordiality. Openness to others' experiences builds openness to others' perspectives, and such openness provides learning

opportunities otherwise unavailable. When the facilitator encourages participants in a protocol to "hear all voices," it is really a call to highlight a sufficient
number of perspectives on the issue or problem at hand such that everyone
can gain the possibility of new insight. It is also a call to pool knowledge and
thus become smarter in the aggregate, to cultivate and rely upon what Lauren
Resnick (1987) calls shared cognition, which she properly distinguishes as
the hallmark of most complex work situations (McDonald et al. 2007, p. 16).

Not every teacher will intuitively resonate with these points, though
we think that many online teachers will. This is not necessarily because
they are conversant with contemporary research on learning, but because
they cope on a daily basis with the challenging fact that the learning
group is not usually visible to their students—indeed not tangible at all
without the teacher's express intervention. In face-to-face environments,
by contrast, even if students are pinned quietly in little desks, they can at
least look around and see others learning (or not). Their resulting sense
of being part of something bigger—of not being the only one to have surrendered personal liberty in the pursuit of some greater benefit—offers
at least some protection from the enervating sense of isolation that the
online learner may feel. Good online teachers know they need to fight
isolation and are often on the lookout for useful ways to fight it, and one
way is to enlist the whole group in the pursuit of universal participation
by means of protocols.

Forcing Different Kinds of Participation

A second and related deep feature of protocols—and thus of protocol
teaching—is the demand for multiple modes of participation. In the Triad
Protocol, for example, participants must play three distinct roles. Allen
and Blythe (2004) note how most protocols exploit the inherent tension
between talking and listening. Indeed, one of the things that newcomers
to protocols often say in assessing their experience afterward is that they
noticed their own and others' talking and listening more than they had
before—a notable metacognitive achievement. We mentioned in Chapter
1 that some protocols famously force people who like to talk to be quieter
than usual, and people who like to be quiet to speak up more. But what
is true of talking and listening is also true—if one looks across an archive
of protocols—of presenting and discussing, of clarifying and probing, of
responding warmly and responding coolly, of sticking to the surface of a

text and diving below its surface, of formulating one's own interpretations and reflecting on others', of staying low-inference in interpretation and engaging in deep speculation, of expressing fears and expressing hopes, and more. There is a kind of participatory stretching—inherently an intellectual stretching—that is programmed into protocol use.

Of course, this stretching, as we suggested in Chapter 1, can be a source of initial discomfort because it segments behaviors that ordinarily flow together, or puts them starkly in juxtaposition. The discomfort is similar to what some people initially feel in online learning too—for example, in threaded conversations where people speak across different time frames and on unusually (from the perspective of ordinary conversation) circumscribed themes; in chat boxes where the power to build a conversation may seem to rely more on typing speed than on thinking; or even in video chats where technical glitches and time lags may impair attempts at more authentic communication. In the end, however, Web-based learners learn that the Web is about associative, nonlinear thinking—that ultimately its power comes from contact not control—and they get used to that. In fact, contact without control may be sufficient for many learning purposes, as Jason Snart (2010) suggests—for example, immersion in a rich informational environment whose exact parameters are unclear. Meanwhile, protocol learners eventually get used to the appositional thinking and behaving that protocols force—for example, giving due respect to both warm and cool reactions, listening for 10 minutes straight before responding, or responding without judging. And learners discover that appositional thinking and behaving are powerful for certain purposes.

Making and Reading Texts

A third deep feature of protocol facilitation and teaching concerns their preoccupation with the making and reading of texts. By *texts*, we mean renderings of thought and experience in any medium. Texts can be spoken accounts, drawings, videos, photographs, and so on (Scholes, 1985).[9] Of course, all signature pedagogies focus on texts. The word *lecture*, for example, is the French word for *reading*, and the original lectures of the medieval universities were readings from manuscripts so rare and valuable that they were actually chained to the lecterns (Streeter, 1931). And, of course, the signature pedagogies of contemporary colleges and schools are full of readings—often from *text*books—and they are full of text making as well. For example, much math instruction includes sharing and discussing problem solutions; and much art instruction includes presenting and critiquing work in progress. And all assessments, by definition, involve renderings of learning (as well as readings of the renderings) in such diverse textual formats as little "blue books," uploaded Word or PDF or Google documents, presentations and exhibitions of various kinds and in various media, and, of course, the ubiquitous bubble sheets.

What is qualitatively different about the use of texts in protocol pedagogy, however, is the frequent treatment of texts *as texts*. Historically—before there was a Web 2.0 or even a Web 1.0—much of the appeal of protocols was that they pressed educators to render their practice into texts, for example, composed accounts of dilemmas or collections of artifacts from their teaching. In just that preparatory phase, the protocols forced unusual and valuable reflection. Then they invited collegial readings of these texts within trustworthy settings, provoking still deeper levels of reflection, as well as collegial learning. For example, there are peer-review protocols that require presenting teachers to assemble a complex rendering of a teaching unit (rationale, goals, materials, assessed student work, perhaps annotated videos of the unit in action, and reflection on its effectiveness).[10] Now, of course, with handheld sound and video recorders as close as one's mobile phone, the task of rendering practice into text is far easier than it once was and, perhaps as a result, less revelatory in itself. Still, the collective reading of a text by others remains hugely valuable—to the text writers *and* readers.

Numerous other protocols are also designed around readings of texts from practice, and they typically follow what is called a semiotic approach. Semiotics is the practice of textual analysis common in literary, media, and cultural studies (Eagleton, 1983; Scholes, 1983). It involves analyzing both the surfaces and deeper features of texts (just as we're doing here with protocol pedagogy). Semiotically oriented protocols include the aptly named Peeling the Onion, as well as Success Analysis Protocol, Rich Text Protocol, the Four A's Text Protocol, and the Text Rendering Experience.[11]

How is this text-as-text deep feature of protocol use relevant to teaching online? Our answer is that the Web is the greatest collection of texts ever assembled, and one of the great affordances of online learning—as we'll explore in Chapter 3—is that it brings every one of these texts within a few keystrokes of every student everywhere. As we know, however, it is one thing to gain access to a text, and quite another to read it thoughtfully. And it is still another thing to read it with the benefit of collective interpretation and even collective action. Hence the value, we think, in exploiting a set of existing tools designed to assist with these kinds of collaborative text use. Moreover, when it comes to web-based teaching and learning, as Chris Jones and colleagues (Jones, Cook, Jones, & de Laat, 2007) point out, collaborative text-based discussion is at the heart of the most commonly used format, namely asynchronous conferencing.[12]

Fostering Trust

A fourth deep feature of protocol facilitation and protocol teaching has to do with trust. The participants of a Triad Protocol, for example, who agree to play what may be an unfamiliar and uncomfortable role, do so because they feel safe in doing so. The safety they count on, however, is more than the safety that every teacher is ethically obliged to provide—for example, from racism, sexism, and bullying. It's more subtle, and somehow deeply woven into the environment and the activity. So, the teacher has not, presumably, simply plopped the class into a Triad Protocol without preparation. There are norms of behavior well established, and they have been consistently enforced to a point where all can reasonably expect that every group of three will follow them; and the norms, not only explicitly or implicitly exclude making disrespectful statements about others and their work, but also include giving each other room to try new things and fail. Moreover, the protocol itself seems trustworthy (in combination, of course, with the norms and the teacher's confidence in his or her teaching)—something about the pacing of it, the fact that all must participate and participate in all three roles, and that the triads manage the process on their own.

Some protocols create safety by disallowing immediate interaction. So the presenter in a Tuning Protocol may not respond to feedback when first given. He or she must wait to take it all in—both the warm and the cool—and thus gains time to decide what parts of it to respond to. In the rounds of the text-based protocol called Save the Last Word for Me, participants offer for comment what may be for them difficult patches of text, but they are enjoined from saying why they offer them, and also from commenting on them in any way until the end—after everyone else's comments.[13]

The kind of trust we are describing here is situational. The immediate goal is not that every participant will trust every other participant *as an individual*, but rather that all will come to trust in the situation that has been collectively designed and developed and will find it productive (McDonald et al., 2007). The productivity is defined in terms of learning, and hinges on the fact that the situation is not *just* safe, but is safe for taking risks. To reach new and complex understandings, people often have to put previous understandings at risk (Bransford et al., 2000). They also have to risk revealing that they do not already know what some people may think they should know (Dweck, 1999). Protocols can make it safe for students to surface their original understandings, to get them out into the open. Students speak and present, rather than just listen and respond. Protocols can also make it safe for multiple understandings to surface and mingle—one of the rationales for a collective commitment to participation by all. At the same time, they make it safe for these understandings to be challenged and displaced. Hence the role of things like probing questions and cool feedback.

For all these reasons, protocols can be very useful tools in teaching environments that are especially diverse in terms of students' background knowledge and academic preparedness. And as it happens, online learning communities tend to be especially diverse in these ways—a natural outcome of their accessibility despite geography and without residence, of the convenience of their asynchronous course designs, and of a downward trend in their costs (Lewin, 2011). Protocols can help teachers construe the typical diversity of the online learning group as beneficial rather than troublesome, and as a useful source of additional learning for all—which indeed much research on learning suggests that diversity provides (Bransford et al., 2000). Protocols can help online teachers exploit this opportunity.

CHAPTER 3

Teaching and Learning Online

Teaching and learning online takes a wide variety of forms in the real world, as we suggested in Chapter 1. In this chapter, we take a tour of this variety in three descriptive stops. All three portray a particular instance of teaching and learning online. They are not utopian scenarios, however. Indeed, in each of the stops on our tour, the challenges involved in using protocols may seem to outweigh the benefits, though we try to even this out in the analysis that follows the tour. One reason for the original imbalance is that each of our stops focuses on projects in an early stage of development. They are all about *going* online—a much more common condition today than being already comfortably online, and, of course, messier. Indeed, the entire enterprise of online teaching, it seems fair to say, is in an early stage of development.

FIRST STOP

Our first stop in the tour of online teaching and learning is one that journalist Anya Kamenetz (2010) portrays briefly in her book, *DIY U* (for "do-it-yourself university"). It involves the experiences of Sarah Stern, a University of Colorado communications major who decided to take an online course in communications while interning in communications in New York City (a world capital of communications). In this case, *online course* means one in which instructor and student are physically distant from each other. Here the distance seems mitigated by the obvious relation of the online course to the student's internship. As it happens here, however, this relation is an ironic backdrop to the story.

It turns out that Sarah's professor taught the online course to her and others principally by means of audios and slides from a previous face-to-face version of the course. Oddly for Sarah, she could hear other students speaking up as she watched the slides, though they were not, of course, students who were taking the course with her. As she put it in her interview with Kamenetz, "So while you're watching the PowerPoint and listening to his lectures, you're also listening to him go off on tangents, and students telling stories, and stuff that was a waste of time, basically" (Kamenetz, 2010, p. 95). Of course, the signature pedagogy of lecture/discussion—a staple of traditional university instruction—is typically at least one-fifth "going off on tangents" and "students telling stories," and this is hardly all a "waste of time." Some teachers—though arguably few—know how to use tangents and students' own stories to connect what they are teaching to the students' previous experiences and current conceptions, and even to uproot misconceptions present or forming. "Let's stop right here," one of these skillful lecturers might say. "Here's a cold call, Kareem: How are you making sense right now of what I'm saying about the difference between 'broadcast' and 'broadband'?" And then, "How do you, Brianna, relate to what Kareem just said?" And finally, "Let me digress for a moment to tell you the story of my own epiphany on this distinction. . . ." Sarah Stern's professor is perhaps a similarly skillful lecturer in a face-to-face environment, but, of course, he was not *present* to Sarah nor she to him—even virtually. The students who seemed present were actually ghosts of students past, though Sarah was the one made to feel like a ghost—unknown to those who seemed present, protected completely from cold calls, barred by dimensions of space and time from telling her own stories, and barred by the technology platform even from seeing the look on her instructor's face as he elicited past students' stories. All she could see, as Kamenetz suggests, were the professor's slides.

We don't learn from Kamenetz's account how this professor happened to "go online," but based on what we know about such matters from many other contexts, the path likely involved someone in an administrative role persuasively citing two fallacies about online teaching—that it's easy to do, and that it involves little more than moving what was previously classroom-based into a course management system like Blackboard (Palloff & Pratt, 2011).[1] Maybe the professor was flattered to be asked to go online, having been implicitly or explicitly invited to make his scholarship and teaching available to a wider audience of students. Currently, MIT and Stanford are both showcasing their faculties in this way—in MIT's case, making courses available in this text-based, downloadable fashion (Markoff, 2012). Some commentators, including Anya Kamenetz (2010), see these moves as the possible emergence of a whole new way of experiencing higher education—a high-octane, do-it-yourself education (Keller, 2011). We say instead that texts of teaching are not teaching in and of themselves, though under the right circumstances they can be useful tools for teaching. And protocols can help. In fact, Sarah Stern's circumstances were nearly right in this respect. We can imagine, for example, how this online course in communications might have been tied to her internship in communication to create what Jan Herrington, Thomas Reeves, and Ron Oliver (2010) describe as an authentic e-learning experience, where the authentic task becomes the primary focus of the entire online course. Furthermore, we can imagine other students taking the course who were also interning in communications—possibly in other capitals of communications like Los Angeles, London, and Shanghai. We can imagine the professor using the text of the old communications course—the audios and slides—as a source of concepts and insights that interns might use to make sense of their internships. And we can imagine a protocol that helps them to talk together about this sense making. It might make reference to an essential question like, how is the real world like and unlike the theoretical world?

But Sarah got none of this. And what made matters worse for her was that neither the professor nor she tried to compensate for the resulting lack of what online teachers call virtual presence. "It was kind of bizarre," she told Kamenetz, that the professor never once communicated with her directly—for example, by email. Although she knew that she could have sent the first email herself, she never did. In fact, many professors who "go online" for the first time tend to overlook the disconcerting impact on students of a loss of physical presence. This is particularly the case, say Palloff and Pratt (2011), if they do so without training or with training in the course management system only and not in strategies for teaching with it. Nor do students themselves necessarily notice at first the impact of the lack of presence; it creeps up on them instead. They may therefore fail to take the important step of speaking up early—a particularly awkward step for many in the absence of a teacher's active reaching out (Garrison, Anderson, & Archer, 2001; Lehman & Conceicão, 2010). Indeed, even in face-to-face settings, students who fail to speak up early in a course tend to seal themselves into more or less permanent silence. But in face-to-face settings—no matter how sparsely interactive—students have at least the advantage of seeing other people in the room. So they see they are not the only ones who have surrendered some degree of personal liberty in order to gain whatever learning and other benefits the course has promised. This is the implicit *deal* that underlies teaching and learning environments tied to diplomas, degrees, or certificates: constraints in exchange for benefits (McDonald & Hudder, 2012). Remaining faithful to this deal while also feeling alone in cyberspace is a major challenge for many online learners.[2]

Meanwhile, though the lectures of the online communications course were offered on an asynchronous basis, the exams were held within a tight time frame. We don't know anything about the content of these exams from Kamenetz' account of Sarah Stern's experience, though the exams were likely conventional ones, administered in a relatively synchronous fashion so as to minimize cross-continental cheating. Thus with respect to assessment also, the course seems the perfect example of a simply transplanted one—ignoring, for example, the potential of asynchronous learning environments to capture and assess learning in action rather than only post hoc. A threaded discussion, for example, as Hamilton and Cherniavsky (2006) point out, is in the end a record in the form of deliberately constructed and focused writing of the participating students' understandings as these evolved.[3] As a device for formative assessment as well as summative assessment, it is unparalleled in the world of face-to-face learning and testing. At least for Sarah, by contrast, the assessment tied to the communications course seems to have been just a great irritant. Twice during exam time, the course management system went down, and all she could do was send an email alert and wait for the exam to come back up.

Despite all this, however, Sarah Stern told Kamenetz that she was pleased with her online course. And we can see in the reason one of the great drivers (other than low cost for the sponsoring institution) of the growth in online learning. The course was simply convenient. It enabled Sarah to knock off a program requirement while also enjoying the much deeper learning experience of a New York City communications internship. Yet the course also affirmed for her a sense that she had already acquired about online learning in general, namely, that it involves distance in more than the usual sense. As she told Kamenetz, "Whenever I have friends who are like, 'Yeah, I think I'm just gonna take classes online next semester,' that was always like the keyword for, 'I'm pretty much dropping out'" (Kamenetz, 2010, p. 96).

SECOND STOP

Our next stop in this tour of online teaching and learning draws on one of the authors' experiences—this time Janet's.[4] One of her first teaching assignments as an assistant professor was to develop and teach a course called Learning Sciences and Technology. At its core, the course was—and still is (though in another format)—about how people learn and also about how to apply knowledge of how people learn to the design of technology-based instruction. Janet created a highly interactive, face-to-face course wherein students worked in teams throughout a quarter. In one activity, for example, she had the teams use chart paper and markers to create large visualizations of the similarities and differences among theories they were studying, and they presented these texts to the rest of the class for feedback. Of course, Janet—being a protocol teacher—used various protocols to guide the sharing and receipt of such feedback—often a modified Tuning Protocol. She used less well-known protocols too. For example, one called The Making Meaning Protocol: The Storytelling Version helped her students uncover the significance of personal stories of learning from childhood. They shared the stories in small groups and raised and answered questions about them. Then they analyzed the stories together to uncover the conditions of learning that likely made the experiences memorable, using these conditions as cues for their technology designs. The students' stories often involved learning experiences that were hands-on and collaborative—traits that happen to be good targets for technology assistance.[5]

Overall, this early course in Janet's teaching practice was well received by her students and fun for her to teach. Then, one day, the administration asked her to convert the course to an online format in order to accommodate different students' schedules. This was, of course, a reasonable request in several respects—not least the fact that the course was about technology-based designing for effective learning and teaching. And Janet was excited by the challenge of going online since she had studied online teaching in graduate school but hadn't until then had the opportunity to do any. In the process of adapting the course to an online format, however—and in a way that may seem inexplicable for an author of this book—Janet dropped the protocols! As it turns out, you may recall from Chapter 2, Joe and his colleagues did the same thing when they designed the online component of the Social Responsibilities course. They didn't think to include the protocols that had proved so effective in the conference component of the course. We can imagine reasons why both of these coauthors slipped up (though neither remembers exactly why). First, they were likely wary of the fallacy we identified in Sarah Stern's story above: One cannot simply move a course whole-cloth from a face-to-face environment into an online one. Online enthusiast David Wiley told Anya Kamenetz (2010) that that's like thinking you can play water polo with the same moves that worked with ponies on the field. Some transformation is always required. Secondly, the coauthors probably had a strong association of protocol-assisted facilitative leadership with the physical presence of the facilitator. Consider, in this regard, the words we have highlighted in the following excerpt from *The Power of Protocols*. Collectively, these exude physicality, though—as all we coauthors realize now—each word also has its online analogue:

> Facilitative leadership is the *lubricant* of democracy in any setting or field. Indeed, its *presence* signifies that what is called democratic in the setting or field is not some old rusty idol, but a living influence in the form of *people at hand* who know how to call a meeting to order and run it, take thoughtful notes and use them to good and democratic effect, respect dissonance and *surface it*, *press* thoughtfully for consensus and negotiate its achievement, keep others on task and civil, use *tension* productively, *mitigate* personal animus, and so on (McDonald et al., 2007, p. xiv).

While this imagery of protocol-based facilitation (*and* implicitly of protocol-based teaching too) is indeed physical, the thing it describes is more the *protocol's* work than the facilitator's. That is, the *protocol* lubricates, surfaces, presses, mitigates, and so on. And one of the reasons why protocols work so well in online settings, is that they can do these things *without the teacher being there*—at least in the conventional sense of *being there*.

But both Joe and Janet had to learn this the hard way. Janet's first move in taking the Learning Sciences and Technology course online was to post texts for students to read, and provide what she hoped would be thought-provoking prompts for a discussion forum on the texts. This is a common move in online teaching, and it often results in what Janet got— namely, an unfocused discussion (Maurino, Federman, & Greenwald, 2007–2008). If Janet didn't check in at least once a day on these discussions, threads turned into webs, with students going off on many tangents. Meanwhile, in her checks, she inevitably discovered some students dominating and others barely contributing at all, and numerous students responding to the overall task with monologue—that is, never adjusting their own contributions to others' (Stodel, Thompson, & MacDonald, 2006; Thomas, 2002). Being there constantly to spot these problems and help resolve them can prove exhausting for a teacher. Janet increasingly felt overwhelmed. This too is not an uncommon experience for online teachers. They sometimes come to feel that they simply cannot keep up with the task of making discussions productive, though they may know that tending to the quality of discussions is a key strategy for providing virtual presence in the online learning experience (Maurino et al., 2007–2008).

Trying to imagine a better way, Janet stumbled back into protocols. First, she looked for a protocol that would help her students see complex topics from multiple perspectives—exactly what her students happened to be studying at this point in this course about learning. In *The Power of Protocols*, she found Save the Last Word for Me, and adapted it as the basis for an online, asynchronous discussion forum for a text about learning in complex domains.[6] In the forum directions, Janet asked half the students at the beginning of the week to post a quote from the text that they didn't quite understand but found, nevertheless, intriguing (a provocative but also liberating prompt and one that calls for a lot of close and thoughtful reading just to find the right thing to post). She told the students that she wanted just the quotes themselves, no other comments. Then, midweek, all students were prompted to post a reaction to at least one posted quote, explaining what *they* thought the quote might mean. Finally, getting the "last word," the original quote posters were prompted to disclose what they had learned from reading the other posts and also to explain what they had originally found intriguing about the quotes. The next week, the other half of the class got to be the quote posters.[7]

After Janet added this to her online class on learning sciences (and some other protocols we describe in later chapters including an online version of the Making Meaning Protocol that uses the virtual world of Second Life), she saw some dramatic improvements in her students' learning. And she found some as well in her daily workload—indeed, enough improvement in both respects to suggest the need for a study. Thus, she and her colleagues Aimee deNoyelles and Kay Kyeong-Ju Seo began a systematic study of the use of online protocols in asynchronous discussion forums. As reported in their article published in *Computers & Education*, they found students taking more ownership of the discussions and learning how to facilitate the discussion themselves—without the teacher interventions that Janet had previously thought necessary (Zydney, deNoyelles, & Seo, 2012). Protocols decrease teacher interventions in online discussions because they force participation, and shift focusing responsibilities to students themselves. Save the Last Word for Me, for example, is not only highly directive in terms of when to post, but also about the content of the post—though without constraining creativity. Indeed, as we argued in the previous chapters, the directedness of protocols typically enhances creativity. So it is also with the directedness of games, as we suggested in Chapter 1, or with the directedness of many art forms.

Janet and her colleagues also found in their study that forums guided by protocols were easier to read. They displayed neat threads in rows. In the case of the Save the Last Word protocol, for example, each thread included a short description of the selected quote with two responses followed by a final response titled "Final Word." The forums without the protocols resembled a tree with branches going off in many different directions, often representing different tangents and making it difficult to determine who was responding to whom. Meanwhile the researchers found that the protocol-based forums increased overall student interaction. In particular, they noted fewer student monologues. Students told the researchers that they appreciated how the protocols made other students' thinking visible, and caused them all to pause and reflect more on the texts they were reading and discussing (Zydney et al., 2012).

Freed from reading burdens and from the need to intervene on issues of focus, online teachers may gain time to intervene on issues of understanding. Once she turned (back) to protocols, Janet found that she was able to help more students who needed her help and was also able to attend more to the crucial role of harvesting themes from the discussions.

THIRD STOP

We begin this stop in our tour of online teaching and learning with two framing references. The first reference is a story from the *New York Times*. A photo that accompanies the story shows 7th-grade science students sitting in a "digital classroom" in Munster, Indiana, in rows of typically middle school desks with an open laptop on each. "Laura Norman used to ask her seventh-grade scientists to take out their textbooks and flip to page such-and-such," the article begins. "Now, she tells them to take out their laptops." Later, reinforcing our sense of the pedagogical inertia implicit in the photo, the chair of the middle school math department is quoted as follows: "The material we're teaching is old, but everything around it [namely the technology] is brand new" (Schwarz, 2011, para. 4).

Our second—and contrasting—framing reference is an online survey of 55,000 U.S. students as part of NetDay 2004. The students were asked to imagine how technologies of the future might help kids learn. They imagined something quite different from what the Munster, Indiana, students got some 7 years later. Here is what the analysts of the survey findings call a modal response:

> Every student would use a small, handheld wireless computer that is voice activated. The computer would offer high-speed access to a kid-friendly Internet, populated with websites that are safe, designed specifically for use by students, with no pop-up ads. Using this device, students would complete most of their in-school work and homework, as well as take online classes both at school and at home. Students would use the small computer to play mathematics-learning games and read interactive e-textbooks. In completing their schoolwork, students would work closely and routinely with an intelligent digital tutor, and tap a knowledge utility to obtain factual answers to questions they pose. In their history studies, students could participate in 3-D virtual reality-based historic reenactments. (U. S. Departments of Commerce and Education & NetDay, 2004, p. 6)

Again, this was 2004, before iPhones and Androids and the nearly complete eclipse of mobile phones by handheld devices that can not only phone and text, but take pictures, make movies and recordings, search the Web, tell you how to locate pizza, and much more. This was also early in the development of online learning systems as well as online publishing. It was 3 years before the Kindle, 6 years before the iPad, 7 years before the voice-activated iPhone 4. And it was early in the currently energetic effort to create new pedagogical practices based on games, animations, and simulations (Gee, 2007; Plass, Homer, & Hayward, 2009). Yet all these elements seem prefigured in what the NetDay responders had to say. Of course, that should not be surprising, since anticipation of technology tools—often promoted by popular media—significantly precedes their arrival. And when such tools do appear, as intelligent tutoring systems in math had already done by 2004, they may exert a hold on the imaginations of possible users that exceeds their actual power. The NetDay kids might today express considerable disappointment with how intelligent digital tutors have actually been incorporated into schooling. The sometimes-heralded School of One, for example, seems to us less like what the NetDay kids imagined and more like the platoon system that was an early-20th-century innovation— still mass-production schooling, but with an individualized facade.[8]

On this third stop of our tour of online teaching and learning, we explore an alternative to the Munster, Indiana, version of Web 2.0

schooling—one that seems to us more like the version of Web 2.0 school-ing the NetDay kids imagined. Our hosts on this stop are University of California, Berkeley, Professor Glynda Hull and her research and teaching colleagues around the world. Collectively, they have built a global network of "out of school" Web 2.0 learning environments. Each environment is a blended one—part face-to-face and part online. The network overall is distinguished by what Hull and colleagues call three *freedoms*:

- freedom from everyday identities—particularly ones that arise from and are often frozen by school environments
- freedom to exercise intellectual agency, especially to choose one's own intellectual projects
- freedom to move while learning—literally to walk around from one physical space to another, rather than be confined by class blocks, and classrooms, and rows of small desks—and also to project images of oneself into worlds beyond one's immediate environment (Hull, Kenney, Marple, & Forsman-Schneider, 2006).

At this stop, *going online* has a different relationship with *distance* than in the two previous stops. Here the teacher and students occupy contigu-ous space. However, Web 2.0 tools afford students an opportunity to in-habit distant space too, where they encounter young people different from themselves with whom they exchange representational texts about their lives. The medium for exchange is an intranet that Hull and her colleagues created and support, called Space2cre8.[9] It is what the NetDay kids de-scribed—namely "a kid-friendly Internet populated with web sites that are safe, designed specifically for use by students, with no pop-up ads." Space2cre8 mimics the functionalities of MySpace and Facebook—for ex-ample, the opportunity to form a friendship network; to make wall and blog postings that use music, pictures, and video as well as words; to send private messages; and also to participate in groups and chats (Hull, Consul-tancy protocol, & Sahni, 2010).

The network is called Kidnet, and the face-to-face learning environ-ments are in the United States, India, South Africa, England, and Norway. Kidnet also involves a distributed network of researchers who use semiotic methods to explore the texts that kids create on Space2cre8. We used this term *semiotic* in Chapter 2 also, referring there to a characteristic use of protocols to examine closely the surfaces and depths of student work and other texts drawn from educational practice. Semiotic text rendering, commonly used in literary, media, and cultural studies involves a kind of "peeling of the onion" as in the protocol of the same name.[10]

The texts that Kidnet participants share often take the form of what Hull and her colleagues call digital stories, or multimodal compositions, which typically situate their authors not only in their present communities and identities but also in what James Paul Gee (2007) calls projective identities. These are ones the kids try on for various developmental reasons—for example, in order to test their interests, to sustain their optimism in the face of adversity, or to imagine new lives. For example, Shushma, a 17-year-old living in a poor village in India and standing firm against the demands of her family to give up her ambitions to be a teacher for a premature marriage, decorates her Space2cre8 homepage with the picture of a rainbow and a photo of a famous Indian actress. Meanwhile, Anthony, a South African boy chooses an image of Lil Wayne, the American rapper, though a distant Kidnet friend challenges him: "Why don't you post your real picture?" And he eventually does (Hull, Stornaiuolo, & Sahni, 2010).

Hull, Stornaiuolo, and Sahni (2010) refer to Kidnet as a networked set of "sites for cosmopolitan practice" (p. 331). Cosmopolitanism is a contemporary philosophical movement that aims to help 21st-century people open themselves to the often startling cultural differences that surround them and to regard these as sources of learning (Appiah, 2006; Hansen, 2010). Within Kidnet, as Hull, Stronaiuolo, and Sahni (2010) put it, cosmopolitan practice involves, on the part of the Kidnet authors, a turn from *self-work* (writing about their lives and projecting their identities into others' imaginations) to *other-work* (coming to terms reciprocally with these other people's lives and imaginations).

Space2cre8 does not by itself provoke cosmopolitan practice. However, it offers unusual and creative access to intercontinental, intercultural, and interreligious contact (for example, between rural Hindu Indian kids and urban evangelical American kids). Whether the contact proves productive for learning depends especially on what happens in the face-to-face learning environments that support it. Do they provide the scaffolding sufficient to provoke and support what Hull & Stornaiuolo (2010) call the necessary "dialogue and the respectful imagining of others across aesthetic, cultural, historical, and ideological difference" (p. 86)? This is not an easy teaching task—as any teacher who has ever attempted it knows well—but protocols can help, and on at least one Kidnet site, they have begun to.

The New York City Kidnet site is called the EXCEL Academy. Funded by the Teagle Foundation, and run jointly by NYU and the Children's Aid Society, the Academy enrolls high school students from two South Bronx high schools, Fannie Lou Hamer High School and Explorations Academy. It convenes periodically in the South Bronx and on the NYU campus during the school year, and then intensively at NYU for 3 weeks in the summer. It was designed to provide participants a rich precollege experience in the context of scaffolded cosmopolitan encounters—between the South Bronx and Greenwich Village (including cheap lunch food available in the respective neighborhoods), between high school and college, and—by means of Space2cre8—between New York and other parts of the world. The Academy was co-founded by Hull (as a site for cosmopolitan practice), by ethicist David Velleman of the NYU Philosophy Department (as a place to teach logic to high school students as grounding for general philosophical inquiry, using an online game he developed called blogic), and by one of us, namely Joe (as a bridging device for NYU and its South Bronx partner schools and also as a place for using protocol pedagogy to teach cosmopolitanism). We name these diverse purposes to suggest that innovation in education often incorporates diverse purposes. However, successful innovations find ways over time to connect the purposes.

In the several years since the launch of the EXCEL Academy, and under the direction of Anna Smith, there is evidence that its students have integrated the founders' different interests. For example, they seem to understand the connections among eating what to them are strange foods like sushi and falafel during their daily advisory lunches in the summer, exploring the iMovies of kids who live on the other side of the world, learning the fundamentals of logic, and learning to learn with protocols.[11] For their part, however, the adults involved have been a little slower to understand these connections—a common theme across all our stops and a sign of early development in each case. A good example of the lag here has to do with the use of a protocol Joe created called the Cosmopolitan Protocol. It uses Peter Elbow's (1986) methodological believing and doubting to press participants to withhold judgment in the face of culturally strange encounters.

Within the Cosmopolitan Protocol, the facilitator asks participants to *believe* in some facet of a strange world [represented in a text of some kind]—for example, that a mother might commit an "honor killing" of her daughter, or that a nation might ban an important form of religious expression. The *believing* is not necessarily genuine. It is merely a way to "get inside" the other culture in order to get used to it—to begin to understand it better. Participants are asked—either in a go-round or by volunteering—to share a comment that derives from this effort to *believe*.

In teaching with the protocol in the EXCEL Academy, however, Joe used news clippings as texts, never thinking to use rich findings from Kidnet research of actual cases of intercultural encounter—for example, Shushma's stand-off with her parents and Anthony's projective identity as Lil Wayne, both mentioned above. Nor did Joe direct EXCEL students to find their own texts in Space2cre8, even though they moved directly from his class to their Space2cre8 lab. Finally, he never asked them to use what they were learning in their blogic class each morning in order to think in a systematic way about difference and our ethical obligation to come to terms with it.[12]

CHALLENGES OF GOING ONLINE

The preceding tour of online teaching and learning in only three stops is admittedly like a tour of the whole United States in three stops—say, the Grand Canyon; Washington, D.C.; and Disney World. Still, it does illuminate some challenges that we think are pervasive. Here we explore three of these challenges more fully: the lingering challenge of access, the baffling challenge of inertia in ordinary educational systems and ordinary practice, and the critically important challenge of achieving presence.

Access

Access to the rich online teaching and learning we espouse continues to be limited for a variety of reasons that include the geographical differences in the distribution of bandwidth, and the inability of individuals, families, and schools to afford the continual hardware update and maintenance costs of 21st-century technologies.[13] This is true not only in developing countries—like some of the ones where Kidnet operates—but also in the United States. Moreover, access issues are not just physical. Some are matters of design and psychology. Certain software and interfaces and course management systems do a better job than others in inviting and enabling access or in dealing with access issues that may arise (Conole &

Oliver, 2007). Some intuitively designed tools fit certain people's intuitions better than other people's. Some people get cognitive overload and become navigationally disoriented amid the associative learning dynamics typical in Web use, the toggling among texts and windows of texts, and the threads of asynchronous learning formats (Wang & Gearhart, 2006). Some teachers are good at recognizing such problems and helping people get past them, and others are not. Some learners exhibit patience in the midst of access issues (remember the story in Chapter 1 of how we authors kept slogging through our first difficulties going online in the writing of this book), while other people (or the same people, including us, at other moments) seize up with impatience and even rage.

Inertia

This is a theme of all the stories. It explains what may seem to the reader the incongruous disconnection between Sarah Stern's university-arranged internship in communications and her online course in communications. While universities tend to be inclined to incorporate online coursework, they are enormously resistant to accommodating real change in pedagogical practice. This should not be surprising. Although we rightly associate universities with innovation, they are also conservators—not just of pedagogies (which elsewhere rise and fall with more regularity), but of ideas, cultures, art, history, and more. Thus universities innovate mostly on the edges, for example, in Silicon Valley spinoffs or in individual professors' funded projects like Kidnet. And even in innovative projects like Kidnet, the regularities of the university may be hard to budge, for example, the disconnection between what happens in one class and what happens in another. Similarly, while we may rightly think of schools as chasing innovation (for example, in Munster, Indiana), pedagogical inertia is the continual backdrop for the chase. It coopts technological innovation to such powerful regularities as curriculum "coverage" and student surveillance and control.

In both higher education and K–12 settings, inertia is the combined drag of many forces: space, time, expectation, and the tradition of deeply entrenched pedagogies, which may, for example, equate teaching with moving and talking, and learning with sitting and listening. A key question is how to deal with inertia in these various circumstances, and here we see hope on all our stops. One can, as Sarah Stern does, point out in vivid detail to people like Anya Kamenetz how an innovation fails to deliver what it might but, meanwhile, make the most of it: take advantage of the convenience it affords, get comfortable inside it, and someday perhaps help tip it toward a new state. Or, as Janet and her colleagues do, one can work directly to make the innovation deliver more of what it promises—in their case through pedagogical innovation. Finally, as Glynda Hull and her colleagues do, one can work wholly outside the system, though with an eye to making subversive change within the system. And one can, as Joe does in his Kidnet-related teaching, acknowledge inertia as a key step toward overcoming it.

These are all ways of engaging in what David Tyack and Larry Cuban (1995) call "tinkering toward utopia." For these authors, neither *tinkering* nor *utopia* are derisive terms, except when separated as, for example, when reformers are too directly assaultive in their reform efforts—we might say blindly utopian, playing too much the role of social engineer—or when they are tinkerers without vision. Seymour Papert writes in his 1997 review of Tyack and Cuban's book that it helped him understand that reform of complex systems requires *evolutionary* change but, at the same time, confirmed for him that complex systems are vulnerable to evolutionary pressure—namely, to the creeping (one might say tinkering) impact of the introduction of diversity.

Presence

Presence is, of course, a major theme of our first stop—where it is notable in its absence within Sarah Stern's experience. But it is there too in Janet's experience, which reveals the ways in which presence needs to be re-imagined for online environments—away from dependence on direct teacher intervention, and toward accountable social networks. Finally, presence is an issue in Glynda Hull's work—in fact, the core issue of her cosmopolitan intentions: how to be present to others who are different, and how to touch and be touched by difference without simply acquiescing to it. The issue of presence is also there in the question of how to help kids who are strangers to each other in so many dimensions to become present to each other in some other dimensions.

How to achieve presence in online teaching and learning is a much addressed question in the online professional development literature. For example, Rosemary Lehman's and Richard Berg's 2007 book with the daunting title *147 Practical Tips for Synchronous and Blended Technology Teaching and Learning* is all about presence. The authors' exhaustive list is a reminder of all the things that face-to-face teachers sometimes take for granted, but online teachers must explicitly plan for, given the distances they continually seek to bridge. For example, they have to think about how they will manage to see and hear their students on the first day and ensure that the students see and hear each other. Online teachers also have to plan how to monitor interactions, since many of these happen beyond their direct notice.

Rene Palloff's and Keith Pratt's (2011) book, *The Excellent Online Instructor,* also deals substantially with the problem of achieving presence in the face of distance. For example, they advocate "the formation and support of communities of practice among faculty" (p. 54). They also suggest that the whole learning community be "the vehicle through which the course is effectively conducted" (p. 9). In other words, they urge a shift in the balance of power—from teacher as sole content source, prime facilitator, and chief planner to students themselves. In an earlier (2005) book, they spell out how such a shift might be achieved, namely, by commissioning teams of online students to create "charters" or consensus-derived documents that spell out, for example, how their teams will identify themselves, how they will communicate, even what day of the week their communication will begin. Very protocol-like, we thought, when we read about these charters. Indeed Palloff and Pratt's writing overall is one of the primary sources of our sense that there may be a hunger among some excellent online instructors to discover protocols.

BENEFITS OF GOING ONLINE

Yes, there are challenges in going online—indeed even more than are revealed on our tour's three stops. But the crucial question for this book and for educational practice is whether the benefits outweigh the challenges. We think they do. In our final bit of analysis here, before turning to descriptions of online protocols in the next four chapters, we assess these benefits. In doing so, we revisit each of our stops in turn. There we find benefits that we call prospective, pragmatic, and strategic.

Prospective Benefits

Sarah Stern's experience offers a good opportunity to understand what we mean by *prospective* benefit. Of course, she derived real and present benefit from going online, but the benefit was modest. She got convenience—enough for her to tell Anya Kamenetz (2010) that she was happy she had done it. Taking the course online enabled her "to pick up the extra course credit while pursuing her future career goals" (p. 95). This is faint praise, however, given the fact that the online course was in communications and so were her career goals. She surely had a right to expect more. On the other hand, the convenience of the extra credit may perhaps have played a crucial part in persuading her to take the New York internship in the first place, which for a Colorado communications major may well have proved life changing or, at the very least, a good resume booster.

If that's not enough to justify the challenges, however (and we think it's not), here is the *prospective* view. What if, in subsequent summers, and possibly as a result of Kamenetz's mini-exposé and even our own examination of it, the University of Colorado manages to figure out how to tie this "extra course credit" to internships—and not just for New York interns but for ones in other far-from-Colorado or even within-Colorado places? This would address a persistent mistake that both universities and schools make with regard to incorporating various kinds of field experiences into the curriculum—namely, leaving it up to students themselves to figure out the connections between what they learn in their internships and what they learn in their courses and other on-campus experiences. Although universities and schools sometimes offer or require students to take internship-support seminars, these do not help much in our opinion. In most cases, they become just another campus-based experience. And, of course, Sarah Stern would not have been able to have an internship in New York if she had had to take a campus-based support seminar as well—two thousand miles away. Moreover, field supervisors are very expensive—impossibly so where distances are great. But even in more proximate internship sites, field supervisors can prove ineffectual by being too rarely present. Going online, we think, is the only sensible way to address the problem—though not by simply repurposing a lecture-based course as happened in Sarah Stern's experience. Imagine instead offering field-based learners frequent synchronous or asynchronous opportunities to share texts with each other that they themselves draw from their field-based learning. These might be uploaded videos and other images, accounts of dilemmas, brief case studies, and the like. In the online company of a teacher who is deeply knowledgeable about theory *and* practice, the students would work to make sense of these texts by the light of what they have also learned in coursework and other on-campus experiences. Indeed, the online learning could be captured in texts like ones that are featured in Stern's story—recorded lectures (but viewed in brief segments as in the Khan Academy[14]). Of course, a protocol could assist them in this intertextual examination, for example, adaptations of a number of those described in the rest of this book (say, the Success Analysis Protocol in Chapter 6).

Pragmatic Benefits

In our second stop—focused on Janet's taking her protocol pedagogy online—we emphasized the benefits of online teaching with protocols. Here, we want to use the same stop to discuss the benefits of online teaching in general (with or without protocols). We call these *pragmatic* benefits to associate them with the pragmatics of teaching, for example, taking attendance, making assignments, grading assignments, structuring time for planning and learning, giving individualized attention, differentiating instruction, and keeping students on task.

We think that Janet's experience is a compelling (if challenging) invitation for all teachers to take their practices online. Here we don't just mean whole courses, as Janet did, but also parts of courses. For example, many higher education teachers today use Blackboard or other virtual learning environments (VLE), though often for only limited pragmatic purposes, for example, text storage. So, the VLE is the place to find the updated syllabus, the required PDF reading, or the link to some other reading. Similarly, increasing numbers of K–12 teachers are using platforms like Google Docs or Dropbox, though again for only limited pragmatic purposes, for example, to collect student work and to stay in touch with who is doing what work and when. Yet these technologies afford so much more.[15]

Here is Janet's quick take on what going online has added to her teaching and her students' learning:

- Students have more time to reflect and respond in the asynchronous environment. For example, in responding to each other's work, students get extra time to consider their feedback rather than having to offer it on the spot. This especially helps shy students and students with native languages other than English.
- Janet has more time to facilitate and respond.
- Janet has opportunities to correct or redirect students off-line, for example, the student who mixes warm and cool in the same comment, or otherwise makes mistakes in postings, or the one

who seems confused. An email suggesting he or she modify a post saves potential embarrassment.

- Janet has opportunities to delete an inappropriate comment (often inadvertently inappropriate) before it does potentially great damage. She does not do this often, but she appreciates being able to do it. Once someone says something inappropriate in a face-to-face setting, she says, it is impossible to delete, and can at most be corrected or softened.
- Students have opportunities to exploit a much wider variety of texts as learning resources—literally millions of them, all a browse away, and well beyond those that Janet may tag. They include photos, videos, animations, games, historical documents, and other media.
- Students have opportunities to respond to each other and to reflect on their learning (as well as illuminate it for assessment purposes) in a far greater range of expressive modes: podcasts, videos, blogs, wikis, slides, and more.
- Both teacher and students have opportunities to travel together to exotic locations, for example, to hang out together in Rome or travel through the human heart—thanks to Second Life.[16]
- Learning and the learning community extend beyond the confines of a single classroom and certain hours of the week.

Strategic Benefits

Our third stop affords us the opportunity to think about what we call the *strategic* benefits of going online in teaching. These help us tinker toward utopia, that is, make moves that help evolve ordinary educational practices (Tyack & Cuban, 1995). Hull and her colleagues make several excellent tinkering moves. First, they are ambitious in their use of technology, using high-end Web 2.0 tools that involve text production as well as communication and implicitly tie learning to settings where such tools emerge, for example, technology labs, adventurous worksites, and advanced social networking sites. At the same time, their deliberately constructed "out-of-school" settings escape much of the inertia of school themselves. Second, Hull and her colleagues surround their efforts with research, indeed, in a manner that rivals those of technology developers. As in technology development, the Kidnet researchers work at least partly within the tradition of design research, whereby design development intersects closely with design documentation and impact study—in this case on learning, identity development, and ethical development (Collins, Joseph, & Bielaczyc, 2004; Hull, Kenney, Marple, & Forsman-Schneider, 2006). Third, Hull and her colleagues hitch their enterprise to the accelerating integration of cultures worldwide—one of the great phenomena of the early-21st century (Suarez-Orozco & Suarez-Orozco, 2002). And they do so ambitiously, connecting Oakland, the South Bronx, rural India, inner London, Muslim Norway, and rural South Africa. Finally, the Kidnet project positions itself with respect to school reform at a perfect strategic advantage—not as frontal assault, but as brave counterpoint. K–12 reform initiatives, most significantly the effort to establish a set of national or Common Core Standards, are obsessed with literacy but, say Beach, Hull, and O'Brien (2011), with a literacy stuck in a "uni-modal, non-digital, decontextualized, test-directed, and teacher-centric" conception (pp. 161–162). Kidnet's contrapuntal efforts sew diversity that can in time propel evolutionary change.[17]

CHAPTER 4

Online Protocols for Starting Up

Online teachers and face-to-face teachers share some of the same challenges when they open or launch courses and other learning experiences. One is that they need to create connection among their students—a sense that they are present among each other, share a common set of learning goals, and are more or less equally committed to achieving these goals. A related opening challenge is that they need to equip their students with a realistic sense of the territory ahead and the demands associated with traveling there. Learning communities can fall apart quickly absent a sense of connection and a realistic expectation of demands.

Protocols can be helpful in addressing both of these teaching challenges, and often at the same time. There is, for example, the protocol called Marvin's Model. In face-to-face versions of this protocol, the teacher asks a small set of questions that preview key ideas of a course, and students in small groups answer the questions in fairly quick go-rounds.[1] The result is that before the course is even 15 or 20 minutes old, everyone has had the chance to talk and be listened to on matters deeply relevant to what they will be learning. Crucially too, everyone has met and interacted with three to five fellow students.

Of course, in an asynchronous format, an online version of Marvin's Model might require as much as a week to pull off. Still, we think the time spent is worth it. Indeed, we recommend that teachers spend at least a week or even 2 or 3 at the start of an online course on what we call starting up protocols—ones that enable learners to meet and interact, to feel connected in terms of goals and interests, to begin to engage with the learning work at hand, and to begin to appreciate the diverse strengths that they and their fellow students collectively bring to the work. We think such experiences are necessary precursors to the kind of protocol-aided online interactions that we call *delving in* (and that we explore in Chapter 5). Ultimately, a learning community capable of delving in, of using its diverse skills and intuitions to help everyone advance in understanding, has to be built by doing real learning work together in shorter bursts. And that's what starting up protocols support.

As we hope you already know or will soon discover, however, protocols are quite versatile tools, and many can be put to *starting up*, *delving in*, or *finishing up* purposes. Still, this chapter describes some that are especially good openers.

A HINTING GAME

We learned about A Hinting Game from Donna Schnupp, an instructional designer for Johns Hopkins University School of Education's online courses in education. Donna based it on a simpler Get to Know You activity. It is good for launching early forays into content, for establishing community, and also for encouraging a culture of playful exploration that may persist and catalyze later *delving in*.

Purpose

The fundamental purpose of the protocol is to help students get to know each other, but it can have powerful content-related purposes too, as explained below.

Details

The protocol is typically used in the first week of an online course, and it involves a threaded discussion forum. Depending on the technology required for step 1, it may require some side coaching there. It is most effective with groups of 10 to 20 students; however, teachers of larger classes can assign students to smaller groups for the purpose of the protocol.

Steps

1. *Profiling and hinting.* At the beginning of the week, students compose profiles of themselves as threads in a discussion forum. These profiles might include professional interests or experiences, leisure interests, and personal facts, but they have to end in a hint of something interesting and undisclosed. Students can choose their own means of hinting, for example, via quotation,

image, phrase, story, or link. To enhance the content learning opportunities of this first step and to encourage creativity, originator Donna Shnupp requires students to post their profiles using an online presentation tool that may be new to them, for example, Prezi, Animoto, Photopeach, or VoiceThread.[2] For the same reason, Janet, who has adapted this protocol to her teaching, requires that the hinting be related to the topic of the course. In her Learning Sciences course, for example, she asks students to hint about their own learning preferences or their favorite learning theorists. She provides a list of theorists for students who are unfamiliar with any. This gets these students immediately exploring background material via Web searches.

2. *Connecting.* During the middle of the week, students choose at least two other students with whom they "connect," that is, whose profiles they perceive as overlapping or complementing their own. They respond to these students in posts that identify a basis of connection and also attempt to guess the substance of the student's hint.

3. *Revealing.* At the end of the online week, all students reveal the substance of their hints, as replies to their original thread titled "Reveal." In this reply, they also say why they presented the hint as they did (for example, in a quotation, image, phrase, story, or link).

4. *Reflecting.* Finally, in a reflection thread posted by the teacher and within the same timeframe as the last step, students post a reply debriefing the use of the protocol.

In the final step, students often say that the protocol's simple steps helped them to get to know one another. Indeed, by then, students have typically ended up posting responses to many more students than required. Meanwhile, the game-like quality of the protocol seems to foster connections that stick and that can be used for deeper learning later. Moreover, if students have learned a new presentation tool along the way, or have hinted about and then discussed their interests related to course content, they have already made tangible learning gains.

REFLECTION ON A TERM

The starting-up protocol Reflection on a Term is inspired by Patricia Carini's child study protocol called Descriptive Review of a Child. A facilitator of a Descriptive Review sometimes begins the review by focusing on a word chosen with the child in mind (Himley & Carini, 2000). Aimee deNoyelles, a doctoral student at the University of Cincinnati from 2007–2011 and now an instructional designer at the University of Central Florida, adapted this idea for online environments.

Purpose

The purpose of the protocol is to help students get to know each other. But it also stimulates course-relevant prior knowledge and associations and makes them available for use, adjustment, or displacement.

Details

This protocol takes an online week to facilitate and can be done on any platform that allows students to post and comment on pictures. Aimee uses Ning,[3] but even threaded discussion forums could be used.

As with A Hinting Game, the Reflection on a Term protocol works best in groups up to 20, though teachers of larger classes can easily adapt it for subgroups of students.

Steps

1. *Assigning the term.* The teacher picks a term that is central to the course and also complex. It can be "loaded" in the sense that people may bring different and even conflicting interpretations to it. In her original version of the protocol, Aimee deNoyelles used the term *educational technology*.
2. *Pondering and choosing.* Students are asked to ponder the term, then choose one of the mental images they have conjured up in their pondering.
3. *Representing.* Students next search on the Internet for a visual or auditory image that corresponds in some way to their mental image, or they create their own corresponding image with a digital camera or a drawing or audio tool.
4. *Posting.* Students post their images, and cite where the image came from (if they didn't create it themselves). They also comment on why they chose the ones they did. This posting is due toward the

middle of the week to give everyone a chance to find or create an image.

5. *Reading and reflecting.* Students read each other's images and reflect on at least two that resonate with them (taking care as a group to ensure that everyone gets at least one reflective comment). This response is due at the end of the online week.

Aimee has found in using this protocol that her students choose images related to their interests and also to their personalities. For either reason— or perhaps just because an image trumps words—the images they choose lend the choosers an online presence that helps others relate to them and remember them. This is crucial for later efforts to work together and delve together more deeply into content. Indeed, when Janet uses the protocol, she adds a step incorporating a collage she creates of all her students' images. In this step, the students are asked to participate in a discussion of the themes that seem to them to cut across the images.

POSTCARDS FROM THE EDGE

The opener Postcards from the Edge is a favorite of many face-to-face protocol facilitators, including Alan. In the face-to-face version, protocol participants are typically given picture postcards, often composed of black-and-white photographs. Some facilitators distribute the cards randomly, while others place them all face up and ask participants to choose one. In any case, the facilitator then poses a question that aims to link the post-cards imaginatively to whatever learning work is at hand. For example, a facilitator may ask, "How does the postcard reflect your experience with professional development?" Or he or she may ask, "How does the postcard reflect your experience in collaborating at work?" In online adaptations, however, the teacher doesn't need to invest in acquiring an expensive collection of postcards and can go well beyond black-and-white photos.

Purpose

Like other opening protocols, this one aims to introduce students to each other and thereby lay a basis for future and deeper learning. The protocol also aims to help students experience the power of multiple perspectives.

Details

As in most of the other opening protocols described in this chapter, teachers of online classes larger than about 20 students might want to subdivide the class for this protocol. The subdivided groups might then become customary work groups. The protocol works on any platform that allows easy sharing and commenting on images (Edmodo, for example[4]).

Steps

1. *The collection.* The teacher locates and downloads an appropriate number of images (roughly one for each person) and posts them, citing sources. The images may all be visual, or some may be visual and some auditory (for example, a whimper, a howl, a grinding noise—anything likely to provoke associations). Or the images may be both visual and auditory as in short video clips. Like the black-and-white postcard photos often used in the face-to-face version of this protocol, the images selected for the online version should have an ambiguous quality.

2. *The assignment.* Next, the teacher directs students to the images and a question. The teacher may randomly assign an image to each student (or to pairs of students to increase collaboration and dialogue), or he or she may ask students to view the entire collection of images and select one to which they are drawn. The question the teacher poses should deal with the learning goals at hand, for example, "How does your image help you think more deeply about educational technology?"

3. *Identification.* Students identify their images and explain in a comment why they chose them. They do this within a day or two of the teacher's initial prompt. The goal here is spontaneity.

4. *Reflection.* Students are asked by the end of the online week to read each other's comments and to add a reflection on what they have learned from the protocol about the course topic.

FEARS, HOPES, AND NORMS

It is very important to set norms and expectations at the opening of every course or other learning experience. The Fears, Hopes, and Norms protocol, adapted here for online use, is a particularly bold and energetic way to do this. The boldness is in the open expression of fears and hopes concerning the kind of environment participants want and need. And the energy comes from the collective effort to devise and carry out plans to ensure that hope wins out.

Purpose

The purpose of this protocol is to surface the expectations students have regarding a productive learning environment and to establish group norms designed to meet these expectations.

Details

The online version of this protocol should take no more than a week in an asynchronous environment and can be done in well under an hour in a synchronous one. Any platform that allows people to edit the same document simultaneously can be used. Google Docs works well, for example, because it allows the creation of a document with two columns—one for fears and one for hopes. This protocol works best for groups of less than 20—otherwise the lists quickly become redundant and hard to read. However, it can be adapted for a larger group by subdividing the group.

Steps

1. *Expressing fears.* The teacher posts the following question (in the left column of a page):

   Fears: If this course turns out to be one of your worst ever, what will be its characteristics?

   Students are given 2 days to respond. They should be encouraged to post only one or two fears until most others have posted, but may then add an additional one or two. They should also be encouraged to look over the list before posting and avoid restating any fear already on the list. Posting should be anonymous. If the protocol is synchronous, however, 15 minutes is sufficient for the posting, plus time for everyone to read the final list. It is crucial in this case, however, that the synchronous platform provide continuous document updates and not require refreshing the screen.

2. *Expressing hopes.* The teacher posts the following question (in the right-hand column or in a separate area if the platform provides no columns):

> *Hopes: If this course turns out to be one of your best ever, what will be its characteristics?*

Students are given 2 days to respond. They should be encouraged to post one or two hopes. After most others have posted, they may then add an additional one or two posts. They should scan before posting and not repeat. Posting is anonymous. If done synchronously, 15 minutes is sufficient time for this step. If done asynchronously, the teacher may combine this step with the previous one and allow posting of fears and hopes at the same time. In that case, however, students should be encouraged to post an equal number of each.

3. *Transitioning to norms.* The teacher posts the following question in a separate area:

> *Norms: Considering our fears and hopes, what agreements can we make to decrease the likelihood of realizing our fears and to increase the likelihood of achieving our hopes?*

It may be helpful to provide students with an example of a norm and in a format that the teacher thinks will be helpful and easy to remember. Students are given until the end of the online week to respond in an asynchronous format, or they are given 15 minutes in a synchronous format.

4. *Synthesizing norms.* After everyone reviews the final list, the teacher synthesizes the norms listed with an eye to both the fears and hopes expressed. This step is best done in an asynchronous way—giving the teacher time to fashion a set of norms that not only takes the students' input fully into account but also honors the teacher's sense of what is needed. In synthesizing, the teacher takes stock of the fears especially and makes sure that they are indeed dealt with in the norms. For example, if there are fears related to tech support, is there also a norm that addresses it? If there are fears concerning feeling isolated or falling behind, what norms address these? The synthesizing may involve grouping related items or rephrasing them as needed to aid understanding and memory (though it's important too to use students' original

wording as much as possible). Some norms need concrete elements that only teachers are in a position to supply but that are needed to assuage students' fears. For example, fears about technology challenges are best addressed not only with an assurance of continuous tech support (if available), but with a number to call to activate it. The teacher has huge discretion in this step, but should wield it thoughtfully and with explanation—for example, about why he or she either added or deleted a suggested norm. The teacher should also provide students the opportunity to offer friendly edits before the norms are finally adopted. Once adopted, however, the norms are prominently posted on the course website and frequently referred to by the teacher and (in the best circumstances) by students too.

Facilitation Tips

Less is more when it comes to norms; and short, positive, aphoristic ones hold longer in memory. Instead of saying "No multitasking during synchronous sessions," for example, a norm might say, "Take a break from multitasking when you go online." McDonald's doesn't post rules about disposing of your own trash, it just writes "Thanks" on the lids of all trash receptacles.

Teachers who use subgroups or teams (as recommended in many of the protocols described in this book, particularly for larger groups) should require the teams to set their own norms. These team norms should cover such concrete matters, for example, as how often members should check the forum, and how the team will rotate various roles (facilitator, note taker, and so on). After all the team norms are set and posted, the teacher should consider the elements they have in common, then—adding a few additional ones as needed—he or she should develop and post a set of overall course norms.

PROVOCATIVE PROMPTS

Provocative Prompts was developed by Nancy Mohr and Alan Dichter. In their professional development work together, they often used quotations to stimulate discussion and help participants surface and express opinions and disagreements. Janet adapted the protocol for use in her online graduate course on the learning sciences. In this course, Janet uses the protocol to help students imagine and consider different perspectives on a topic under discussion. By reading and reflecting on quotations that illuminate different perspectives, her students become more comfortable disagreeing with each other, and they can use this comfort to form more easily their own opinions and challenge more easily others' opinions. This makes the protocol a formative one in terms of building course culture. At the same time, the quotations inform students' discussions of whatever content topic is at hand.

Purpose

This protocol helps promote a course culture that considers disagreement as productive for learning. It encourages the development of different perspectives on a topic under consideration, and at the same time informs discussion of the topic.

Details

The Provocative Prompts protocol takes an online week to facilitate and utilizes a threaded discussion forum. Although it is probably better for use with smaller classes (or with subgroups of larger classes), this protocol can be adapted for groups as large as 40 by picking enough quotes to allow for about five or six responses per quote.

Steps

1. *Organization.* Prior to the online week, the teacher creates a new forum on the discussion board where he or she posts the quotations—each within a thread whose title is the first few words of a quotation. Directions to students are to find one quotation that resonates and one that irritates. The aim is to surface agreement and disagreement.
2. *Initial posting—agreement.* Students post a response to a quotation that resonated with them and explain in the post why it did. They title this response "Agreement." This posting is due mid-week.
3. *Initial posting—disagreement.* Students post a response to a quotation that irritated them and explain in the post why it did. They title this response "Disagreement." This posting is due mid-week.
4. *Final posting.* By the end of the online week, participants read through all replies to both the quotations that resonated and the ones that irritated. They then post a reply to a new thread posted

by the instructor titled "New Insights." Here they share any new ideas they have gained as a result of reading other students' perspectives on the quotes.

Facilitation Tips

For this protocol to be successful, it is critical to pick a set of quotations that features a variety of perspectives and that is likely to prompt a variety of reactions. That is why the protocol is called Provocative Prompts. But this is hard to pull off. For example, the first time Janet used the protocol, almost all her students agreed and disagreed with the same quotations—hardly a good feed for the discussion she had planned. To deal with the problem, however, Janet played devil's advocate on both sides, and that helped. Students themselves can play devil's advocates too.

Variation

One advantage of online teaching is that it can employ different media. Thus, an alternative to using print quotations is to use video or podcast ones instead.

THE MAKING MEANING PROTOCOL:
VIRTUAL ENVIRONMENT VERSION

The Making Meaning Protocol, created by Daniel Baron, is widely used in face-to-face settings to explore texts. In Chapter 3, we discussed one adaptation of it for online teaching, and here is another. In this adaptation by Aimee deNoyelles, the focus is not a text in the usual sense, but a virtual multi-user environment called Second Life. In Second Life, which is animated, immersive, and three-dimensional, one can meet others (real others, though represented by animated avatars), and together with these others or alone, one can explore a variety of places. The places may be unique to Second Life, for example, a singles club, a virtual tattoo parlor, or Cape Serenity Library, which houses a collection of writings by authors with disabilities; or the places may be virtual versions of places that have a real historical or contemporary counterpart, for example, ancient Rome, the inside of a human cell, the city of Bucharest, or Arkansas State University, where one can take an online course.

When teaching a course on educational technology issues, Aimee used Second Life to explore various dimensions of learning and technology. But initially, as she told Janet one day, she experienced difficulties in facilitating her students' Second Life explorations. When she gathered them together there, her students' avatars sometimes fell into silence, and sometimes they started speaking simultaneously. Janet confessed that she too had experienced teaching problems in Second Life. Once, for example, one of her students' avatars came to Janet's seminar attached to a bottle of bourbon. Using a virtual currency that is bought with actual dollars, visitors to Second Life can purchase things—including liquor—which then attach to their avatars. This student had purchased his bourbon just before class and couldn't figure out a way to detach from it. What he didn't know is that attachment to bourbon in Second Life (in imitation of real life) leads to virtual intoxication. When he showed up in class, he spewed purple elephants all over the classroom, which disrupted Janet's lesson. This was one of the events that persuaded her to use protocols in her Second Life teaching—including a norm-setting opener that includes a warning not to mix Second Life drinking or clubbing with Second Life learning. Janet suggested that Aimee use protocols also to address her Second Life teaching problems, including the Making Meaning Protocol.

When Aimee first used this protocol to explore such sites as Explorer Island, Guadalajara, and the Storybook Deli, she divided her students into small groups and assigned each one a facilitator and a particular site to explore. However, she found that the facilitators, still getting used to Second Life themselves, could not easily facilitate too. Janet, in her use of the protocol, keeps the large group together, and hers is the variation we describe below.

Purpose

The purpose of the Making Meaning Protocol: Virtual Environment Version is to help students gain basic familiarity with the Second Life environment, though only after they have first gained basic Second Life navigational and communication skills.

Details

Janet facilitates this protocol in a 1-hour synchronous session in Second Life, offering everyone enough time to explore a designated environment as a group and then discuss their findings. In order to participate in the protocol, students must have downloaded Second Life (for free), created an avatar, and entered the environment at least once on their own in order to experience navigating and communicating there. This protocol is best done with small groups of 10 to 12 students. In a large online class, the teacher can schedule separate sessions for small groups.

Steps

1. *Preparation.* Prior to the first meeting in Second Life, the teacher should choose one or more places there for the group to explore, as well as a meeting spot for a follow-up discussion, for example, a virtual classroom setting. As he or she might in a face-to-face setting, the teacher should arrange the chairs in a circle in the virtual classroom.
2. *Introduction.* The teacher emails students directions for the protocol along with time and location for the meeting, as well as advice for learning how to access and begin to understand Second Life.
3. *Presentation.* At the beginning of the meeting, the teacher explains the purpose of the protocol, briefly describes the place or places that everyone will explore, and gives a time and place for a follow-up discussion.
4. *Exploration.* Students explore the designated places for 15 minutes and take notes on what they experience. Then they meet with the teacher in the designated discussion space.
5. *Description.* In a go-round, students describe their exploration in a low-inference way. What did they see? What did they hear? What did they do? The teacher cautions against higher-level inference, whether interpretive or judgmental.
6. *Questions.* In a go-round, students raise questions based on their exploration.
7. *Speculation.* Here the ban on interpretation is lifted, and students speculate—again in a go-round—about aspects of the space they have just visited and briefly explored. The teacher may follow up any or all contributions with a question about the evidence on which the speculation rests.
8. *Significance.* The teacher asks the question, "What is significant or meaningful about this place [in terms of the learning goals of

the course]?" For example, Aimee deNoyelles asks her students to discuss in a go-round the significance of the place they have visited in terms of their own learning or how they might use it with their own students.

9. *Reflections.* For the last round, everyone reflects on what they have learned from the protocol.

Facilitation Tips

With Second Life, as with all synchronous communication, there is a high probability of technical problems, especially with newer users. One tip is to ask everyone to arrive 15 minutes prior to the start of the meeting to troubleshoot as needed. Another is to provide protocol directions in an email sent prior to the visit and to ask students to keep a printout handy. Finally, if feasible, the teacher may wish to have a technical assistant on call to address tech problems that may arise during the protocol.

A unique teaching problem associated with Second Life is that students can become distracted by the environment itself. For example, once Aimee sent her Making Meaning group to explore Second Life's Mexico and arranged for the follow-up discussion to happen at a beach located there. However, the discussion was frequently interrupted by a passing donkey cart and "hee-haw" sounds. Hence, the recommendation above to schedule the discussion for a virtual classroom.

Second Life allows mixed modes of communication. In a protocol-based live-chat, students can use either voice, texting, or both. Managing both, however, can be distracting for users unaccustomed to mixed modes, and hard on facilitators. We recommend starting out in one mode or another, and if texting is the choice, assigning more time since texting takes longer. Moreover, we recommend being very explicit in describing how the go-round will work, as the teacher cannot simply motion with her eyes who will begin the round. So, she might say, "We will begin the go-round with the person to the right of me and then the next person to the right will go, and so on." The teacher may also ask the students to avoid talking over one another's comments (if using voice) by standing their avatars up when speaking, then sitting them back down when finished.

CHAPTER 5

Online Protocols for Delving In

In Chapter 4, we presented protocols for starting up online courses and other learning environments, that is, for connecting students with each other and for establishing expectations and culture. With connections, expectations, and culture in place, online protocol teachers can take learning deeper, for example, engage students in significant problem solving and text analysis, widen or challenge initial conceptions and perspectives, and press for synthesis. We call all this *delving in*. The protocols presented here lend themselves well to delving in, though, being versatile, they can be used for other purposes too.

SAVE THE LAST WORD FOR ME

The Save the Last Word for Me protocol, originally developed by Daniel Baron and Patricia Averette, is a variation of the Final Word protocol (described in McDonald et al., 2007). The variation is designed to help students confront and unravel mysteries and other difficulties they encounter in challenging texts. As described in Chapter 3, Janet adapted this protocol for use in her online graduate course on learning sciences, where students encounter complex theories written in academic language they may not be accustomed to reading.

In that class, for example, students read articles on cognitive flexibility theory by Rand Spiro and others (Spiro, Collins, Thota, & Feltovich, 2003; Spiro, Feltovich, Jacobson, & Coulson, 1991). This is a complex instructional theory involving the use of multiple perspectives to help learners understand difficult topics, and students often have difficulty understanding it. For this reason, Janet has found that they are often uneasy about sharing their interpretations of what they read. This causes some of them to lurk (in online lingo, to fail to contribute actively to group learning), while it provokes others to dominate. In the process, some important elements of the text may be overlooked. Save the Last Word for Me helps correct this effect.

Purpose

The Save the Last Word For Me protocol encourages students to zero in on passages of texts that they find puzzling or otherwise challenging. Then, in a game-like way, it compels everyone else in the group to risk interpreting the selected passage, but offers time to think. Everyone gets clearer about the text as various interpretations emerge without engaging in debate or premature conclusions along the way. Thus no one is put on the spot for what may be a misinterpretation. All misinterpretations are presumed to be steps toward clarification. In the end, "the last word" spurs reflection and synthesis. And even if puzzlement remains, its dimensions are more avowed than might otherwise be the case and, thus, easier for the teacher to address.

Details

This version of Save the Last Word for Me takes 2 online weeks to facilitate and was developed for use in asynchronous discussion forums with class sizes up to 20 students. When she facilitates, Janet divides her students into two groups, with a different group playing the posting role each week. One way to adapt the protocol for larger classes is to subdivide classes into groups as small as three or four, with directions for all group members to post and reply over a 1-week period.

Students must have online access to the texts that will be discussed in the forum, and the online directions must provide them enough time to read the texts prior to posting their first comments in the discussion forum. The teacher may also want to include a separate Questions forum about the directions. This generally cuts down on additional email.

Steps

1. *Organization.* Prior to the first online week, the teacher should create a new forum on the discussion board with a title identifying the focus of the text, for example, cognitive flexibility theory.
2. *Introduction and selection.* The teacher posts the directions for the protocol along with the instructions for the week. In these directions, the teacher assigns half the students to complete the first postings, explaining that the other half will contribute the first postings in the second week of the protocol.

3. *Presentation.* The posting students select brief text passages that intrigued them and that they think may be important to a full understanding of the text. The passages should be two or three sentences at most and may be as brief as one sentence. Students are urged to pick passages that are complex and/or ambiguous and to not shy away from ones that seem just plain puzzling. This is part of the invitation to take interpretive risks in this protocol, as is the teacher's direction to *not reveal* the reasoning behind the selection. This makes it safe to risk posting a passage that one has not already figured out. Each post becomes a new thread within the forum. The posting students title the thread with the first few words of the selected passage so that participants can quickly see which passages have already been chosen. The directions call for posters to choose passages that have not already been selected. The thread begins, of course, with the complete passage selected (along with a citation that enables responders to put the passage quickly in context, for example, the page number of a PDF file or a quick link to an online page). This initial posting is due 3 days into the start of the online week to give everyone a chance to read the text.

4. *Reactions.* All students (including the ones who contributed the passages) reply to at least one other student's passage. In their replies, they provide an interpretation of the passage, for example, what they think it means, and why they think it matters to the meaning of the larger text or topic. The reaction directions allow for tentative responses—part of the overall risk taking. For example, a student might say, "I'm pretty stumped by this, but I think I'm going to say that this is about. . . ." The teacher who monitors the reactions encourages students to pick passages to react to that have fewer than two responses already, so that everyone who posted receives at least two reactions. The reaction posting is due 2 days after the initial posting.

5. *Last word.* The students who selected the passages finish the first week's round by revealing their original interest in the passage— why they picked it to begin with—and also what they have learned from reading the reactions to their passage and how they will apply this learning. Note that they are not expected to supply a definitive meaning. Typically, however, their "last word" responsibility encourages them to read the reactions carefully and, indeed, to work

on figuring out the passage as thoroughly as they can, including browsing for help from other texts on the Web. The last word posting is due at the end of the online week. Each student posts this as a reply to his or her original thread and titles it "Last Word."

6. *Round repeats.* The entire protocol is repeated the following week with the other half of the class posting passages selected from either the original text (if not sufficiently illuminated as a result of the first round) or a related one.

Facilitation Tips

There are several potential problems that can arise in a running of Save the Last Word for Me. One is that multiple participants, despite the warning, may select the same passage. To prevent this from occurring, the facilitator can monitor the discussion forum and email any participant who posts an already-posted passage, asking him or her to delete the posting and create a new thread with a different passage. Or the teacher might ask the student to delete the posting and just write an additional reaction posting. It is better for the facilitator to make such corrections by email or instant message, so as to avoid potential embarrassment to the student. A second potential problem is that the initial posters may not remember that they also have to reply to another poster's passage. The teacher should monitor the discussion forum to make sure that they do. As with all protocols, however, most participants get the hang of this one after a first try, and second and third tries generally go smoothly (and thus require less intervention, which as we pointed out in Chapter 3 is not true of more open discussion threads). Finally, a third potential problem is that students may not post in a timely manner or not post in a way that spreads reactions across all the passages. It is discouraging to have to write a last word on a passage that lacks a sufficient number of reactions. Here, the teacher's monitoring can help, but so can his or her deliberate effort to develop an accountable social network among the students—to point out that this protocol works only when everyone comes to understand the text more fully and that this goal is everyone's responsibility. One of the great advantages of the online version of Save the Last Word for Me is that everyone in the class can read through all the threads and gain, thereby, a considerable scaffold for understanding an otherwise challenging or possibly even baffling text. At the end of the week, the facilitator can encourage everyone to do this by sending a mass email or posting a class announcement. Moreover, the teacher can write a summary posting that highlights some of the major themes touched upon during the protocol— or assign this summary task to students or groups of students.

Variation

We tied the above description of this protocol to word-based texts. However, it's important to note that the protocol is not logocentric despite its name. It can easily be used with complex visual texts also, for example, paintings, videos, or animations (with a system for coding selected "passages," say, subquadrants of a still image, or minutes into a video).

START, STEER, SUMMARIZE

Among educational reform organizations, the New Teacher Center (NTC), based in Santa Cruz, California, but working nationwide, is among the most adventurous in terms of online teaching—having increasingly moved in the last several years from face-to-face mentoring of early-career teachers to online mentoring (using both synchronous and asynchronous formats). Moreover, NTC is a pioneer of protocol-based online teaching. Its flexible and frequently used Start, Steer, Summarize protocol is a good example. Our description of it here is informed by Alyson Mike, director of NTC's online professional development. It is used asynchronously to support mentors through ongoing and rigorous professional development and by the mentors themselves to support their mentees. It is thus a multilevel teaching tool.

Currently, NTC uses this protocol on its GoingOn learning platform, but Alyson says the protocol is flexible enough to be "platform neutral."[1] In fact, it is flexible enough to suit many applications that go well beyond teacher education. In this sense, it is a great exemplar of what we hope this book will do, namely spur imagination beyond the literal recipe. The three moves of the Start, Steer, Summarize protocol are elemental, if nonetheless challenging, teaching moves in face-to-face as well as online situations— *starting* a conversation (or activity) in a purposeful way, *steering* it in ways that explore relevant content in a focused way and with substantial participation, and finally *summarizing* it in ways that promote synthesis and metacognition.[2]

To support mentors' use of this protocol, NTC has prepared a curriculum of prompts to start conversations of various kinds. One kind of conversation might involve references to current research. Having chosen, for example, an article on classroom equity from the NTC curriculum of prompts (under research starters) and having posted it for mentees to read, a mentor might start the conversation with questions about the article, as in the following example: "How do *you* create equity in your classroom by addressing different learning styles, encouraging the participation of underrepresented students, and challenging all students?" Or the mentor's starter might use a research reference without requiring that mentees read it, as in the following example: "I recently read an edition of a National Science Teachers Association journal that includes articles on inquiry across the disciplines [link to journal]. For example, there was one that discussed how to get students inquiring into the factors underlying the rate for dissolving sugar cubes. I'm wondering what ideas *you* have for chemistry inquiry labs." Both these prompts have an intentional content focus and provide clear steering direction—across all three ways of promoting equity in the first example, and across multiple ways of designing for inquiry in science teaching in the second example. Finally, they suggest a useful endpoint, such as answers to the questions, "So what have we learned about general principles of teaching for equity?" or "What patterns exist among these different ways of teaching inquiry in chemistry?"

Purpose

This protocol is designed to facilitate the discussion of a particular, well-chosen, contextualized prompt. As the participants respond to the prompt, the facilitator *steers* the conversation toward the intentional focus and, finally, summarizes or coaches participants to summarize in a way that helps participants retain what they have learned for their ongoing practice.

Details

The facilitator can set the timeframe for the conversation based on whatever constraints and opportunities present themselves. It is best to practice this protocol first with a relatively small group, say, five to ten students if possible. Alternatively, peer facilitators might be identified and oriented by the class instructor. They can then do the steering and also work collaboratively on the summarizing.

Steps

1. *Start.* The facilitator communicates electronically with the participants, explaining the protocol and including any expectations regarding frequency or timeline for participation, and then posts the "Start" prompt as the first thread.
2. *Steer.* As participants respond to the prompt with their reactions, the facilitator steers the conversation back to the intentional focus. In the process, he or she might post another prompt to lead participants toward a deeper consideration of some point and may correct a persistently tangential participant by private email.
3. *Summarize.* Once the timeline for discussion has expired, the facilitator drafts a focused summary, intended as a useful "take-away" for participants' ongoing work, and shares it for time-limited review and feedback. Following the review and appropriate revisions, the facilitator creates a PDF of the summary and posts it in the course archive.

Facilitation Tips

In addition to steering the conversation toward a continuing focus on the starting prompt, the facilitator listens for tone and may jump into the conversation if necessary to maintain a healthy sense of community.

Variations

This protocol, adapted to other contexts, may be used in a blended course in which face-to-face conversation is also possible, in which case the review and feedback process described in step 3 can happen when the class or group members are physically together. The outcome of that discussion can then be the basis of the final document that is prepared and disseminated.

THE PRUNING PROTOCOL

Anne Burgunder, a master teacher in NYU's Department of Teaching and Learning, teaches prospective math educators and supports their student teaching. She also does extensive professional development and consulting, using a variety of face-to-face, online, and blended environments. The

Pruning Protocol, developed by Anne, is designed to be used in a blended course in which the larger group is subdivided into triads.

Purpose

The protocol provides an opportunity for a fairly large group of people to engage with a rich question or problem in a way that alternates spontaneity and play with deliberation and consensus.

You may have noticed that this Pruning Protocol is also a *punning* protocol—that is, the name is a play on the Tuning Protocol. Indeed, it might be said that half of the learning power of the Pruning Protocol comes from the tuning that goes on nearly automatically as small groups share their ideas with each other and adjust their perspectives to what they hear, and then do the same again within the larger group. But the other half comes from pruning—that is, vigorously and successively cutting back to promote better growth.

Details

This protocol can be used with fairly large classes subdivided into triads. The prompt is introduced in a face-to-face meeting, and triads meet either face-to-face or online (synchronously or asynchronously, and via a medium of their choice). The garden "blooms" on a discussion board with forums titled "First Growth," "Second Growth," and "Final Response." The board also contains postings of the prompt and of a rubric detailing expectations for participation. The time it takes to run the Pruning Protocol depends on the challenge of the prompt and also on whether the triads meet synchronously or asynchronously.

Steps

1. *Introduction and "first-growth" ideas.* In a face-to-face meeting, the teacher introduces the protocol, norms, timelines, participation rubric, and prompt. In Anne's practice, the prompt is usually a math question or problem. For example, she might ask, "Which Common Core Practices will you engage in while trying to find the smallest number that has exactly 13 factors?"[3] Students reflect on the prompt in their first triad meeting, which occurs as part of the face-to-face session. Here they do three things: brainstorm approaches to the prompt in a spirit of play, set formats and times

for follow-up meetings (within the framework set by the teacher), and agree on who will take responsibility for which of the three required posts. Following this first session, one member from each triad posts a "first-growth" response to the prompt.

2. *Initial pruning and second growth.* After reading all the first-growth postings, the triads meet to prune in whatever medium they chose during their initial face-to-face meeting. The teacher presses them to take account of other triads' ideas. "These," she says, "give you a richer sense of the garden to come and what it should contain." But paradoxically, she tells them also to "cut stuff back"—telling them that this is what pruning means: "You cut back in order to grow better." Students do this by grouping things, by looking for bigger ideas that subsume smaller ones, and by going deeper. For example, they might read the Common Core mathematics practices and notice that practice 8 involves solving problems of everyday life and realize that finding the smallest number with exactly 13 factors is hardly one of those. A second member of each triad posts the results of its deliberations under the Second Growth forum on the discussion board.

3. *Second pruning and final response.* Once all students have had time to read all the triads' second-growth postings, the triads meet to prune again. The teacher asks, "What new and bigger ideas do you see in all this second growth—ones you want to bring out through your pruning? And, of course, what do you want to give up—that is, to prune?" After deliberation, and within the overall framework of deadlines set by the teacher, the last member of each triad posts a final response to the prompt.

4. *Whole-group discussion.* After reading all the final responses, the whole group meets face-to-face for a final discussion. The material under consideration has now been honed to the point at which discussants are likely to bring deep insights as well as evidence to the discussion. In any case, the discussants will have reached a much clearer understanding of the material.

Facilitation Tips

It may go without saying, but it is crucial that the initial prompt for this protocol (whatever the content) be of sufficient sophistication and complexity that it lends itself to growth and pruning. The teacher should be alert to the

possibility that some triads will have pruned so radically the first time and/
or thought too little about other triads' contributions to make much of the
second pruning. Having a Questions forum available for triads that get stuck
on any step may enable the teacher to help them get unstuck. It may also give
the teacher valuable insight into their learning. We have found that opening
a forum for questions also encourages students to answer each other's questions, fostering a truly student-centered learning environment.

Variation

Although the protocol's name and underlying metaphor is horticul-
tural, Anne's example makes it seem particularly well suited to mathematics—moving students' problem solving from entertaining lots of solution
paths to parsimony. Yet the process is really cross-disciplinary, similar to
the work of a historian sifting through evidence, a musician trying out
chords, or a poet writing a poem. It is possible, however, that the steps of
the protocol may need to be adapted to fit the discipline. For example, the
second pruning in a history class might involve the teacher's delivery of
newly discovered documents.

MARS/VENUS PROTOCOL

This protocol, originally developed by Beth McDonald, was adapted by Janet for use in her blended class on Applying Technology in the Classroom
for Effective Learning. Janet uses blogs, wikis, and discussion forums to extend the learning outside the classroom and to give students an opportunity
to practice the technology skills they are learning. In one of several uses of
this protocol in that class, Janet used it as a forum to discuss the objectiv-
ist/constructivist debate. She had her students read an article by David H.
Jonassen (1991), "Objectivism versus Constructivism: Do We Need a New
Philosophical Paradigm?," and contrast it with excerpts from John Sweller,
Richard Clark, and Paul Kirschner in an edited volume by Sigmund Tobias
and Thomas M. Duffy (2009), *Constructivist Instruction: Success or Failure?*

Purpose

The purpose of this online protocol is to help participants learn from
contrasting points of view, especially when one of the views is less familiar.
In online discussions, students typically summarize course readings. Here,

they must express their own ideas by the light of the different perspectives of contrasting readings.

Details

Although this protocol can be modified to be fully online, the description of it here presumes a blended format. As such, the Mars/Venus Protocol takes 1 blended week to facilitate across an asynchronous discussion forum and a live classroom environment. It works for all sizes of classes divided into small discussion groups of four to six students each.

Steps

1. *Preparation.* Prior to class, the teacher finds a text from a particular point of view for all students to read and forms small groups of students. At the same time, he or she selects two or three short and meaningful excerpts from a contrasting text and posts the quotes in the weekly directions for everyone to read. Then the teacher creates a new forum on the main discussion board called "Mars/Venus." During class, the teacher explains that students will read the article as well as contrasting text excerpts. During the online week, the students will discuss in small groups questions like these: "How do you think the author of the article would respond to these quotations from the contrasting text?" "How do the excerpts from the contrasting text either tap or challenge what you take to be the underlying beliefs of the author we read this week?"

2. *Organization.* Before students leave the first in-person class meeting, they briefly meet in their small groups and decide on the means that they will use to have their discussion (e.g., small group discussion forum, chat, Skype, etc.), and also who will synthesize and post their answers to the teacher's questions in the Mars/Venus discussion forum. Prior to the end of the class, the teacher collects each group's information regarding chosen medium and synthesizer.

3. *Discussion and Synthesis.* After students have read the article and the contrasting text excerpts, they discuss the questions in small groups, in whatever medium chosen. After the small-group discussion, the person who agreed to synthesize the discussion posts the group's answers to the teacher's questions as a new thread in the Mars/Venus forum. This initial posting, titled "Group 5," for example, is due 4 days into the start of the online week to

give everyone a chance to read the assigned text and contrasting text excerpts, and to collaborate with their group members in answering the teacher's questions.

4. *Reaction.* All students reply to at least two other groups' threads, saying whether they agree or disagree with the other groups' analysis and why. This posting is due by the next class meeting.

5. *Final Discussion.* When students come back to class, they meet in their small groups and read through the responses they received to their thread, and prepare a final response to share with the class. Then the class does a go-round where each group shares its reflections on what members have learned from all that they have read—text, excerpts, syntheses, and reactions—and from their small-group discussions.

Facilitation Tips

A key to the efficacy of the protocol is the appropriate selection of texts. They should have strong topical affinity as well as contrast. In most cases, they should also be contemporaneous, though sometimes a contrast in time can work well too, as in the case of the contrast between Jonassen (1991) and Kirschner (2009), Sweller (2009), and Clark (2009). When Janet contrasted these texts in her class, the difference in time got some students to wonder whether Jonassen had kept the same views and prompted them to do further reading that hadn't been assigned.

Variations

As mentioned earlier, this protocol can be run fully online but would need to be spread over 2 weeks. This would provide additional time for the students to decide on their small-group discussion media, and on who among them will synthesize and post. It would also provide additional time for a final reflective posting.

BELIEVING AND DOUBTING PROTOCOL

The Believing and Doubting Protocol pays homage to Peter Elbow, author of the 1986 book, *Embracing Contraries: Explorations in Learning and Teaching.* For Elbow, the key binary code is believing/doubting. *Playing* with these mental states, he argues—trying them on in turn without commitment in order to get the fit of them and in order to consider an issue or a text by their respective lights—is an excellent way to understand ourselves and the world more deeply.

Purpose

Similar to the Mars/Venus Protocol, the Believing and Doubting Protocol asks students to take opposing perspectives on a text. As in debating, "beliefs" and "doubts" are constructed boldly without regard to the authors' instinctive or even considered positions on whatever issues may be involved. And they are posted for all to read in an explicit effort to expand rather than narrow everybody's perspectives. Ultimately, the purpose is that students will emerge from the protocol with richer and better informed perspectives than they might have otherwise adopted.

Details

The texts here can be whole or excerpted and print or nonprint. The teacher posts them as files, links, videos, or podcasts and creates prompts to believe the texts and to doubt them—deeply and serially. Elbow (1986) says that only Jesus and Socrates somehow managed to hold a belief and a doubt in the same instant and that the rest of us have to practice alternating. The protocol takes an online week in an asynchronous discussion forum and works best with small groups of ten or fewer. The teacher can subdivide larger classes.

Steps

1. *Organization and introduction.* The teacher selects and posts the text with an introduction that encourages a spirit of play and explains briefly why the exercise is valuable. At this point the teacher also creates a forum with three threads—Beliefs, Doubts, and Take-Aways—with directions that require that they be taken up in turn according to a strict timeline.
2. *Believing.* At the beginning of the week, all students post a response to the Beliefs thread that makes specific references to the text and argues in support of one or more elements of the text.
3. *Doubting.* Mid-week, students post a response to the Doubts thread that, again, makes specific references to the text, but argues in opposition to one or more elements of it.

4. *Take-Away.* At the end of the week, based on their own reflections and their reading of classmates' posts, students write what they "really think *now*" about the text as a response to the Take-Away thread.

Facilitation Tips

Posting the separate Beliefs and Doubts threads (and insisting that they are completed one at a time) provides an important signal that binary thinking is what is wanted here, not "smooshed-together" monological thinking. The teacher might urge students to "play the game," to "indulge yourself in thinking the absolute opposite of what you may initially think." While the Beliefs and Doubts threads can be dealt with in either order, the Take-Away must come last. It not only signals yet another important turn of mind, but signifies intellectual ownership. Indeed, the teacher should remind students that the prompt is to write what you really think *now*, that is, after the benefit of binary thinking (and reading). For some groups whose members may be tempted to get the Take-Away thread "out of the way" prematurely, the teacher may want to wait until midweek to post that prompt.

Variations

Aimee deNoyelles uses this protocol to have students think more deeply about fair-use guidelines for online resources. She tags a particular set of online videos then asks the students to believe *and* doubt that the videos meet fair-use guidelines. One can, of course, imagine dozens of similar content-focused uses, involving, for example, the trustworthiness of historical accounts or of statistical data sets or the artistic value of various paintings or sculptures.

WHAT DO I KNOW? SUSPECT? NEED TO FIND OUT?

The protocol What Do I Know? Suspect? Need to Find Out? is a variation of a protocol widely used by professional learning communities called What? So What? Now What? (and also a variation of an online protocol described in Chapter 6, The 3 Whats). The prototype, developed by Gene Thompson-Grove, is very useful in situations in which the focus is the complexity of one's own work and learning and where the questions may translate as "What am I really working on?" "Why does it matter to me or others?" and "Where does the work or learning seem headed?" As Alan has concluded, however, Gene's protocol may be a perilous one in situations in which the work is collective and colleagues base their responses to the questions on intuition alone when data is either readily available or obtainable. Hence his variation described below. It aims to shift the emphasis in such situations away from intuition alone and toward data analysis (question 1), hypothesis generation (question 2), and new data generation (question 3). Such a shift can be useful in teaching and learning situations too, particularly wherever a learning goal is to become more data conscious—as it often is in professional education. Thus we illustrate the steps of the protocol with references to an online teaching and learning environment for aspiring school administrators.

Purpose

The purpose of this online teaching protocol, as its title suggests, is three-fold: to take stock of available data (in our illustration, a data set from a single high school, disaggregated by department, teacher, race, gender, socioeconomic status, and feeder school); to generate hypotheses that account for data trends; and to imagine and undertake further investigations. We might well have presented this protocol in Chapter 4—as an early-course stimulus, or in Chapter 6 as a late-course reflection on the need for still further learning. But it works well here too as a guide to deeper delving in.

Details

The protocol takes 2 online weeks in an asynchronous discussion forum and may require some prior training in data analysis. The version presented here is best undertaken in classes with fewer than 20 students, since all students see all posts. However, the protocol can accommodate much larger classes by using small groups to follow the question and reply steps—possibly turning them into synchronous chats—with a final "report-out" posting from each group.

Steps

1. *Organization.* Prior to starting the protocol, the teacher posts all the steps so that students know what's coming. He or she also posts

or provides links to any relevant data sets, for example, in our illustration, the high school data set along with a topical statement that directs the inquiry. For our illustration, this topical statement might read: "This high school has recently been added to the State's list of schools in need of improvement, and our job is to help it improve." Finally, the teacher creates a discussion forum titled "Know. . . Suspect. . . Find Out." This is where the question threads and replies will be posted.

2. *First question and replies.* The teacher posts the first question: "In consideration of this data, what do I know?" Each student posts a reply by the middle of the first online week. Students are encouraged to post only one reply initially, but to keep monitoring the postings, and after everyone else has posted, to post again. Students are also encouraged to build on each other's replies as appropriate (for example, by asking and answering clarifying questions). Thus an early reply might be "I know that passing classes is related to income level," and a later one might be "How do you know that passing classes is related to income level?" That might be followed by "I know that the passing rates in science, math, and social studies are lowest for the lowest income group" and then by "But isn't it possible that the lowest income group is a mostly English language learning group and that this is about language rather than income?" The spirit of this step is to exploit all that the data affords in terms of exploring the topic and to be open to different interpretations of the data.

3. *Second question and replies.* Midweek, the teacher posts the second question: "Based on what we know, what do I suspect?" Again, students are encouraged to respond with only one post initially but, then, after most others have posted, to add another and, again, to build on each others' replies as appropriate. The spirit of this step is to maximize the hypothetical energy. In the context of our illustration, examples of second replies might include: "I suspect that English teachers spend more time getting to know the students through their writing and that they use rubrics to support continuous progress." "I suspect that the African-American boys all come from one middle school and that the math instruction there is not solid." "I suspect that the Asian girls find it difficult to tell the teacher that they don't understand." "I suspect that the science department has a grading policy at odds with the grading

policies in other departments." "I suspect that many families who are sending their kids to this school are experiencing severe economic distress." These posts are due by the end of the first online week.

4. *Third question and replies.* At the start of the second week, the teacher posts the third question: "What do you need to find out in order to confirm or disconfirm your suspicions?" All students are expected to post one item that he or she would be interested in researching/learning more about. These posts are due by the middle of the second online week. In the context of our illustration, examples of third replies might include: "I need to look closely at the feeder patterns and see if there is a correlation with math grades and, potentially, other grades." "I need to find out what the various department grading policies are." "I need to find out if students are actually able to do the assignments given them."

5. *Debriefing.* In the middle of the second week, the facilitator adds a Debriefing thread where all participants write a comment on what they have learned during this protocol, and this debriefing post is due by the end of the second online week.

Facilitator Tips

The empirical emphasis of the protocol is both its great value and its challenge. Calling attention to it along the way can highlight the value and mitigate the challenge. The teacher might say, "We're practicing here for a world beyond this activity, where the genuineness of our questions and the validity of our data really matter. But here—where the stakes are low—we should practice with great deliberation."

CHAPTER 6

Online Protocols for Finishing Up

Protocols can be very helpful in lending a burst of insight and energy to final projects. They can also be helpful in consolidating learning—that is, helping students through reflection and metacognition to take stock of what they have just encountered and learned. Finally, protocols can be helpful in prompting students to apply what they have learned to their lives beyond college and school. The protocols we explore in this chapter lend themselves to all these purposes. We call them protocols for finishing up.

TUNING PROTOCOL

As we suggested in Chapter 1, the Tuning Protocol is one of a handful of seminal protocols. However, it is not typically associated with summative activities but, rather, with formative ones, for example, getting feedback on a proposal or a work in progress. Yet adaptations of the Tuning Protocol have long been used for final assessments and other finishing-up activities, for example, to determine whether a student portfolio meets standards, whether a teacher's portfolio merits a compensation bump, or whether a final draft is ready for publication. The cool feedback that presenters get at that late stage still prompts additional revision, but in a finishing way—as in a dissertation defense, where the faculty committee shakes the new doctor's hand but asks him or her to clean up a few small things before graduation.

In her online graduate course on learning sciences and technology, Janet uses the Tuning Protocol in this kind of finishing-up way—to help her students fine-tune their final project, a design proposal for a technology-based environment (for example, a WebQuest, a learning game, or a multimedia project). The protocol is designed for use in asynchronous discussion forums, but can be used in blended settings too.

Purpose

The purpose of the Tuning Protocol (in this version) is to promote refining and finishing-up energy through peer review.

Details

The protocol takes 2 online weeks to facilitate in an asynchronous discussion forum, and can be done in large classes, with students assigned to groups of four to six. The teacher should specify in the online directions that students will be allowed enough time to read the presenters' work prior to posting their warm and cool reactions in the discussion forum. The teacher may want to include a separate Questions forum for participants to ask questions about the directions for the protocol.

Steps

1. *Organization.* Prior to the online weeks, the teacher creates new forums on the discussion board with a title for each peer-review group (for example, Peer Review Group A). In the description of each forum, the teacher writes the names of its assigned members.
2. *Introduction and selection.* The teacher posts the directions for the protocol. In these directions, he or she explains that the tuning process will take place over 2 weeks.
3. *Presentation.* Within his or her assigned forum, each student posts a new thread with a design proposal attached. The title of the new thread should capture the gist of the proposal. In the posting, the student may highlight any aspects of the design on which he or she would especially like feedback. This initial posting is due in the middle of the first online week, to give everyone a chance to finish his or her designs.
4. *Warm Feedback.* All members of the peer-review group write a warm reply to each design proposal thread by the end of the first online week. They title their replies "Warm Feedback." These attend to the strengths and promise of the presenter's design. The teacher encourages students to share only one warm comment and discourages repeating others' comments. "No need," he or she may enjoin, "to say I agree with what [so and so] said." If a

second warm round seems warranted (given the value of the
first or the enthusiasm that attended it), then the teacher
schedules one.

5. *Cool Feedback.* All students write a cool reply to each person's
thread within their assigned forum. These replies are due within
the same time frame as the warm replies. They title their replies
"Cool Feedback." Cool replies emphasize shortcomings or
problems with the design. The teacher explains in the directions
that cool feedback sometimes begins with wondering, as in "I'm
wondering why you chose to . . ." and "I'm curious about your
decision to . . ." Or it may involve questions, as in "Can you
explain the part about . . . ?" The teacher encourages participants
to provide just one cool comment and warns against repeating a
previous one in the thread. Participants may offer a second cool
reply after the round is over if they have one that has not already
been mentioned and may help the designer finish strongly.

6. *Reaction.* All students reply to their original thread with an overall
reaction to the warm and cool feedback. It should synthesize the
feedback, and also answer the question: What is your current
thinking on your design given the feedback you received? Students
title their replies "Reaction." This posting is due in the middle of
the second week.

7. *Debrief.* All students write a second reply to their original thread,
due at the end of the second week, offering a reflection on the
peer-review process. They title their replies "Debrief." They
respond to the questions: How did it feel to read the warm and
cool feedback? What did you think of the use of this protocol?
Would you use this protocol for your own work in the future?

Facilitation Tips

A few predictable problems can arise in the use of this protocol which
may require the teacher's intervention. One is that students may not know
how to give warm and cool feedback. To help, the teacher may post model
warm and cool comments, for example, with respect to a previous student's
work. A second problem is that one or more students may mix warm and
cool feedback. To deal with this, the teacher should monitor the discussion
forum and email any participant who mixes, asking him or her to modify

the posting. The teacher might also provide students with a checklist for their postings—even one that includes assessment points per element (see sample checklist below). Finally, a problem may be that students fail to post in a timely manner. To deal with this problem, the teacher can monitor the forum and encourage late posters to post.

Sample Checklist

Original Post (5 points total)

- Posted before the deadline (1 point)
- Includes attached design proposal (1 point)
- Includes a title that briefly describes the proposal (1 point)
- Includes questions that elicit responses from participants (2 points)

Warm and Cool Feedback (15 points each)

- Posted before deadline (2 points)
- Posted to all students in your assigned forum (3 points)
- Includes the correct title (1 point)
- Offers an original idea (i.e., strength or weakness) (2 points)
- Contributes just one main idea (2 points)
- Provides an explanation or justification of the idea (3 points)
- Does not mix warm and cool feedback (2 points)

Reaction (10 points)

- Posted before deadline (1 point)
- Includes a correct title (1 point)
- Provides a synthesis of the warm and cool feedback (5 points)
- Includes your current thinking on your design (3 points)

Debrief (5 points)

- Posted before deadline (1 point)
- Includes a correct title (1 point)
- Responds to debrief questions (3 points)

Variations

Having run this protocol in several formats—face-to-face, asynchronously online, synchronously online, and blended, Janet finds that her favorite format is blended. In this variation, she runs steps 6 and 7 (Reaction and Debrief) either face-to-face or in a synchronous format online. Keeping the first part (steps 1–5) asynchronous gives participants more time to review each other's work, to pause and think about the feedback they provide, and to reflect on the feedback they receive; then going synchronous or using face-to-face format for the last part (steps 6–7) enables a richer and more engaging discussion.

THE CHARRETTE PROTOCOL

Like the Tuning Protocol, the Charrette Protocol is often used in online courses to help students move their projects toward completion and in the process gain last-minute quality improvements.[1] At the heart of the Charrette Protocol is the idea that to present work in a charrette is to seek every other participant's ownership, and to respond to work in a charrette is to acknowledge this common ownership. The charrette ethic is to strive to make *our* good work even better.

The roots of the protocol are in architecture and design, but the protocol comes to us via Kathy Juarez's adaptation for education and Funda Ergulec's adaptation for online learning. Pam Rankey's Microcomputer Databases online course at the University of Cincinnati is the setting for the version described below. In her course, students create database designs, and Pam uses the protocol to help them fine-tune them.

Purpose

The purpose of this protocol is to help students improve the quality of their work in its last stages by entertaining others' perspectives.

Details

The Charrette Protocol takes 1 online week in an asynchronous discussion forum, with students divided into small groups of three to six.

Steps

1. *Organization.* Prior to the online week, the teacher divides students into peer review groups of three to six. The teacher also creates a new forum on the discussion board for each group, with members noted in the forum titles.
2. *Introduction and selection.* The teacher posts directions, advising the group of the protocol's ethic: that in a collaborative review of work, the work belongs to all and all are obligated to make *good* even better.
3. *Presentation.* Students post their work as a new thread within their assigned peer-review forum. Within the thread, students ask a question or two about their work by way of inviting particular feedback. The questions can be specific or as generic as "How can we make this better?" or "What is our next step?" Note that the use of plural pronouns in these questions honors the traditional conception of the charrette as common work. This initial posting is titled with a few words to describe the work and is due the first day of the online week.
4. *Discussion.* Students post their responses to each of their own group members' works. In these replies, they answer the questions the owner posed. The emphasis of their answers should be on improving the work, which now "belongs" to the entire group. This posting is due midweek to give everyone a chance to discuss the work.
5. *Summary.* Students read the responses to their initial postings. In a reply to their initial thread—titled "Summary," they summarize the responses and acknowledge new insight they have gained from thinking about them. This posting is due at the end of the week.

Facilitation Tips

There are a few areas where teacher intervention may be needed. The first has to do with tardy posting. To deal with this, it helps if the teacher monitors the discussion and emails as quickly as possible those students who go beyond the posting deadlines. Other common problems include students' failing to ask questions in their initial postings and forgetting to summarize responses in their last postings. Email reminders and monitoring can mitigate these problems, as can strong efforts up front to establish norms. A powerful one is honoring the tradition of the charrette as common work. "What a benefit," the teacher might post, "that everyone gains everyone else's ownership of their work!"

SELF-FACILITATING SEMINAR PROTOCOL

We discussed in Chapter 2 the origins of the Self-Facilitating Seminar Protocol, which was developed by Joe for a course he teaches at NYU's Steinhardt School with a number of other colleagues.[2] This blended course is called "The Social Responsibilities of Educators" and deals with such topics as violence prevention, child-abuse detection, and the creation of safe and supportive learning communities. It combines an all-day conference format on a Friday or Saturday—featuring case studies, films, and protocol-based panel discussions by experts and kids—with follow-up online and in-school hunts for stories and documents and one "self-facilitated" seminar using this protocol.

This protocol is designed to guide small groups of students—in this case, drawn from a larger group that typically ranges from about 100 to about 175—in using social media tools to explore rich and challenging online texts. The Social Responsibilities course directs students to discuss one of two rich texts—both of them interviews of notable scholars discussing issues highly relevant to the course content. The first is University of California, Santa Cruz, feminist and activist scholar Bettina Aptheker, who speaks with NYU professors Robby Cohen and Fred Kaeser about her own experience as a sexually abused child. The second text is NYU sociologist Pedro Noguera, who examines the roots of childhood bullying and proposes responses to it in a conversation with Robby Cohen.

Purpose

The purpose of this protocol is to help students make sense together of Web-based texts that may be complex rhetorically (for example, a long interview about a complicated topic) and that may also evoke emotionally charged responses that groups can help individual participants manage (for example, strong feelings or recollections of child abuse and bullying).

A secondary purpose of the protocol is to help students consolidate and apply what they have learned about the core concepts of a course.

Details

The protocol was designed for a blended format, in which groups connect first in face-to-face and content-focused interaction wherein they make certain foundational decisions regarding membership, leadership, focus, and medium. A theory underlying the protocol is that "self-facilitating" groups need this foundation to handle the challenges of whatever task is at hand, and in order to commit to the task (Baran & Correia, 2009).

In the version of the protocol developed for the NYU course, groups of five to ten students who have shared a table (face-to-face) at a day-long conference (involving as many as 175 students) make a date for further conversation online about one of two videos that go deeper into course content. Each group chooses a video, as well as a leader who agrees to send a date reminder to group members. The leader also agrees to post the documentation of the group's seminar at the course management website. Finally, each group chooses a medium for the seminar. Most choose asynchronous formats (Google Docs, Blackboard threaded discussion, and Facebook, with, in one case, use of a public page to include outside discussants). However, some groups choose synchronous formats (podcast, e-chat, or community podcast).[3] The course puts no limits on media but requires that both threaded discussions and email exchanges be transcribed by the students for easy reading (using copy and paste).

Steps

1. *Prompt.* The teacher posts a prompt for the seminar (regardless of the text chosen)—one that directs attention toward learning goals that the seminar aims to consolidate. In the Social Responsibilities course the prompt reads as follows:

   > You are taking a course designed to teach professionals how to work in socially responsible ways with young people. The learning goals of the course include <u>understanding how to act in a caring way</u>, <u>learning to elicit and listen to students' voices</u>, and <u>believing in resilience and knowing how to foster it</u>. Based on your experiences in the in-person session of the course, any

work you have done to date on the online course exam, your viewing of this video, and any other experience you may choose to cite, discuss the learning goals underlined here.

2. *Guidelines.* The teacher posts guidelines for the conversation and notes that adherence to these guidelines will be the principal basis for evaluation of the conversation. For the Social Responsibilities course, these guidelines are as follows:
   - Make it real.
   - Help everyone speak up in a meaningful way at least twice over the course of the conversation.
   - Pay substantial attention to the video in what you talk about.
   - Pay substantial attention to the course topics and themes.
   - Be respectful of each other, but dare also to be honest and press deeper. Help everyone be honest and take risks by creating a safe and supportive environment.
   - Do your part to ensure that the objective of this assignment is met—namely, that the group and *all its individual members* demonstrate their understanding of the course themes and the video you discussed.

3. *Preparation.* Students review the Web-based text or texts assigned by the light of the protocol prompt.

4. *Groups convene.* Groups convene (by various means) for their discussions. Those who have chosen asynchronous media must set a time frame for beginning and completing the conversation. Group participants work collaboratively to honor the protocol guidelines.

5. *Posting.* The group leader posts the documentation of the group conversation.

6. *Response.* For the Social Responsibilities course, this assignment is one of two final projects, and the only response to the postings is from one of the course instructors who sends an email evaluation to all members of each group. However, one can imagine a final step that gives all students access to all postings.

Facilitation Tips

For this protocol, facilitation tips come in two levels, one for the teacher and the other for the self-facilitating groups and their leaders.

Teacher: It is important that groups not leave the face-to-face setting without providing the teacher with a completed form listing the group's members, its leader (who will act as principal contact), and the seminar medium the group has chosen. Thereafter, the bond formed in the group's face-to-face launch is likely to be strong and to carry it through—with one exception: where the leader proves unreliable. The teacher should monitor leader reliability, for example, by means of emails to leaders asking for progress updates.

Groups and group leaders: Here are the facilitation tips that the Social Responsibilities course offers groups and group leaders:

> The group should agree on a common window of time within which all will watch the chosen video—preferably soon after the date of the seminar. Make sure you read the seminar prompt again just before you watch the video. It's best to watch it in one sitting and to take some notes regarding things you may want to say about it particularly with respect to the prompt. You may also want to note points you disagree with or strongly agree with; questions that arise for you or insights that occur to you; or emotional reactions you have. Once the deadline comes, the group leader should initiate the conversation by throwing out one idea to get it started (avoid long comments with multiple points—they can bog down the conversation). If you've chosen to have an asynchronous conversation (over time via Google Docs or discussion board, for example) rather than a synchronous one (using Skype or live-chat), then the group should agree to stagger its participation. This helps ensure that the participants respond to each other as well as to the video and the assignment. So, for example, Jason and Melinda might join on Tuesday, when they will find Katrina's and Tracey's comments already posted. Then on Wednesday, Tricia can join in, and Katrina and Tracey can return to the conversation. Tricia then gets the final scheduled word on Thursday, but everyone promises to check the final result by Friday and to add anything they want. After the conversation starts, everyone becomes in effect a facilitator. Everybody has the goal of making sure that everybody else joins in and is, literally, on the record in terms of speaking at least twice. The record of your conversation should not be submitted (by the group leader) until everybody listed by name has participated

twice. Note that one of the things the instructor does as he or she reads the record is to count participants' comments. If any fall short, he or she sends a quick email to all the groups' members suggesting that so-and-so "send a final comment and copy us all."

OVERCOMING OBSTACLES

Overcoming Obstacles is a protocol developed by Janet for use in her blended graduate course on applying technology for effective learning. This protocol is loosely based on the Descriptive Consultancy protocol, developed by Nancy Mohr.[4] Janet uses Overcoming Obstacles to help students at the end of her course figure out ways to overcome obstacles to integrating technology into their practice as educators.

The protocol requires 2 online weeks. Janet starts it the next-to-last week of her course in order to give participants enough time to surmise the application obstacles they face, to clarify the dimensions of the obstacles, and to imagine potential paths past them.

Purpose

The purpose of this protocol is to generate energy for putting new learning into practice by means of collaborative conversation.

Details

The version presented here is for use in asynchronous discussion forums but includes variations for use in blended settings. Janet uses this version for groups of up to about 20 students. Bigger groups would likely need face-to-face practice in small groups to start and a format to follow similar to the one in the Self-Facilitating Protocol (see above). In the online directions, the teacher must allow enough time for students to ponder the obstacles the presenters describe prior to posting reactions in the discussion forum.

Steps

1. *Organization.* Prior to the first online week, the teacher creates a new discussion forum with the title of the discussion. He or she

also posts directions for the protocol and directs everyone to the appropriate discussion forum.

2. *Problem presentation.* Each student posts a new thread concerning an obstacle that he or she has faced in applying learning to practice, for example, in Janet's course, integrating technology with practice. Participants title the thread with a few words to describe the obstacle. This initial posting is due 2 days into the start of the online week in order to provide everyone a chance to conceptualize and describe a felt obstacle.

3. *Clarifying questions.* Students read through the problems presented and post a response with any clarifying questions they want to address to the presenters. Answers to clarifying questions address gaps in understanding and fill in missing details. Students title these "Clarifying Questions." These clarifying questions are due 2 days after the initial posting, and presenters should answer them by the end of the first week.

4. *Suggestions.* All students post a response to at least two others' obstacles. In their response, they write suggestions for how this obstacle could be overcome. They title these "Suggestions." This posting is due in the middle of the second week.

5. *Reactions.* All students write a reply to their original thread with their reaction to the suggestions. They are encouraged to share any new thoughts about the obstacles that the responses stimulated. This post should be titled "Reaction." The posting is due at the end of the second online week.

6. *Debrief.* Finally, all students write a second reply to their original thread with a reflection on the problem-solving process. They respond to the questions: How did it feel to write about the problem you were having? What did you think of the responses you received? Would you use this type of protocol in the future for your own work? Participants title their replies "Debrief." This posting is due at the same time as the "Reaction" posting.

Facilitation Tip

This protocol tends to run smoothly with few interventions, though monitoring for timeliness and attention to directions (for example, how many suggestions to make) is always important.

Variations

If the protocol is used in a blended class, then steps 6 and 7 (the Reaction and Debrief) can be done in class or in a synchronous online format, thus affording participants key respective benefits of asynchronous and synchronous meeting formats. The asynchronous first part (steps 1–5) gives students time to assess obstacles in their practice and choose the best one to present, while the synchronous final part (steps 6–7) affords a richer and more constructive discussion. It also cuts down on the numbers of posts the protocol requires, though the teacher should warn students that face-to-face or synchronous sessions always demand a greater degree of advanced preparation.

SUCCESS ANALYSIS PROTOCOL

Many protocols examine problems, dilemmas, or obstacles. This one, to the delight of most participants, examines success—but to an equally powerful effect in terms of learning. The Success Analysis Protocol provides an opportunity for participants to learn from their own as well as each other's successful practice and, at the same time, to reach a greater understanding of what success entails and what its factors tend to be.

Joe tends to use this protocol near the start of a course or professional learning experience, as a kind of warm-up for the often more emotionally challenging work of examining problems, dilemmas, and obstacles. However, Janet and Alan tend to use it at the end. They like what it affords in terms of reflection and summing up. Beth splits the difference. She likes to encourage the perhaps reluctant participant of a workshop in school leadership by suggesting that the workshop will build on his or her success, but she knows that it may be hard for students to conjure up a relevant story of success at the very beginning of a course. So in deciding where to place the protocol in this book, she voted with Janet and Alan.

The Success Analysis Protocol was originally designed by Daniel Baron and was modified for online use (asynchronous or blended) by Funda Ergulec.[5]

Purpose

The purpose of the Success Analysis Protocol is to engage students in collaborative analysis of successful cases of practice in order to understand what makes them successful and to apply this understanding to future practice.

Details

The Success Analysis Protocol takes 2 online weeks to facilitate. Preparation requires dividing the overall group of students into small groups of three to six each and, also, thinking through a coaching side-plan for several demanding steps. The steps we present here are from the asynchronous version.

Steps

1. *Organization.* Prior to the first online week, the teacher assigns students to groups and creates new forums on the discussion board for each group, titled, for example, "Success 2: Derek, Holly, Dan, & Nadia."

2. *Introduction.* The teacher posts directions for the protocol. These should include the reassurance that the success referred to does not have to be dramatic—that people can learn a lot even from small-scale success. The directions should steer clear of the word *case*, as in "a case of success." Although that is what is needed in fact—an account of success that can be puzzled over—*case* can sound intimidating to the ones writing it up; better to use the word *story* instead, as in "a story of success." And the teacher should issue a call for informality: "This is not a literary assignment; the story doesn't have to be polished; you can use bullet points," and so on. Finally, the teacher should recommend that students include references to what they or others, or possibly environmental conditions, might have contributed to success, and be much less concerned about providing evidence that the experience actually was a success. There is no need to cite proof, as in "95% of the class passed the exam."

3. *Presentation.* All students post their "stories of success" in as much detail as they can recall, though with some overall word limit. This initial posting is due 2 days into the start of the first online week to give everyone a chance first to prepare his or her story. Students post the story as a new thread within their assigned group forum. They title the new thread with a few words of orientation to the

story—like "getting the class to listen" (for a student teacher) or "mastering puff pastry" (for a student chef).

4. *Posing questions.* All students read each story posted in their group's forum and pose either clarifying questions (about things they need to know before they can respond) or probing questions (to push the storytellers to unpack their actions further or say more about an aspect that seems crucial to success). Students post these questions within 2 days of the story's posting. Storytellers answer all questions by the end of the first online week.

5. *Reflection.* Once the answers to questions have been posted, all group members offer their insights into the nature and sources of the success recounted in the other group members' stories. This response to the story threads should be posted in the middle of the second online week and titled "Reflection."

6. *Response.* By the end of the second online week, all storytellers respond, writing the response as a reply to the original thread, titling it "Response." They say whether and how their sense of the nature and sources of their own success has shifted and also what they have learned from the protocol about success in general.

Facilitation Tips

It sometimes helps students new to this protocol to have the teacher share his or her own story of success. It gives the students a better idea of the scope of what the teacher is seeking—both in content and format. The story that Janet uses when she facilitates this protocol within her graduate course on educational technology is as follows:

When I was a graduate student at NYU, I took a class where we had to create a documentary video. I worked with a group of two other students. This was an intense project involving many nights and quite a bit of arguing, but *good* arguing—helpful in deciding what we wanted to cover. We ended up creating a documentary about discrimination and violence toward minorities. It was a topic we were passionate about. At the time, the homophobic murder of Matthew Shepard in Wyoming had just occurred, and there were many demonstrations and marches in NYC. We filmed the marches and watched firsthand the violence, particularly by police. One officer rode over a man with his horse. It was awful. We also interviewed several men with firsthand experience of violence and discrimination. Their stories were haunting. The documentary got the stories out, and in a way that captured the feelings and emotions that swelled at that moment of history.

One predictable challenge for many student participants in this protocol, one that a teacher's model story can help address, is to know the right level of detail for the presentation—enough to tantalize, not enough to swamp. Another is how much analysis to include—not so much that it seems to cover most of the ground, just enough to provoke others' analyses. In terms of the reflection step, a predictable challenge involves sticking to the prompt: to offer insight into the nature and sources of the success. The teacher can provide further helpful prompts in the directions or in coaching emails: "How would you describe this success?" "What caused the success here?" And so on. At the same time, the teacher redirects students whose reflections are merely congratulatory or that offer advice for follow up.

Variations

If this protocol is used in a blended class, then steps 5 and 6 (the Reaction and Debrief) can be done in class, rather than online. Or, for online classes, these steps can be done synchronously.

THE 3 WHATS

The 3 Whats protocol is Janet's online riff on a face-to-face protocol developed by Gene Thompson-Grove called What? So What? Now What?, which was created to help participants reflect on their work at whatever duration or level. The What? question becomes "What have I accomplished?" or "What am I working on?" The So What? question becomes "Why does this work matter to me or others?" And the Now What? question becomes "What do I do next?" or "How can I build on what I've learned?"

In Janet's online version, the focus shifts to a course nearing completion and a search for consolidation of learning, reflection on its value, and attention to how it might be applied in the future. The steps below describe the asynchronous version.

Purpose

The purpose of this protocol is to give students an opportunity to reflect collaboratively on what they have learned in a course nearing completion and, in the process, to consolidate that learning and get it ready for application to new settings.

Details

The 3 Whats protocol takes 1 online week to facilitate in an asynchronous discussion forum. Janet uses it with groups of up to 20 students, but using the protocol with somewhat larger groups is feasible too for the version described below, as are adaptations that involve subgroups.

Steps

1. *Organization.* Prior to the online week, the teacher creates a discussion forum titled "The 3 Whats." Within the description of the forum, the facilitator should include the first two questions:
   - *What?* What have I learned in this course? What are the big ideas?
   - *So What?* Why is the learning important? Why do these ideas matter?
2. *Introduction.* The teacher posts the directions for the protocol and directs everyone to the discussion forum.
3. *Presentations.* Each student posts a thread to the forum that answers the What? and So What? questions. Students are encouraged to focus on different elements in their postings in order to achieve breadth, and to indicate this focus in the title of the thread. This initial posting is due 2 days into the start of the online week to give everyone a chance to reflect on at least one big thing they learned.
4. *Now What?* All students post a response to at least two others' initial threads. In this response, they make suggestions about next steps—how to make the most of what they say they have learned, how to apply it. These responses are titled "Now what?" and are posted 2 days after the initial threads are due.
5. *Reaction.* All students write a reply to their original thread with their reaction to the suggestions received as well as their own ideas

for what to do next. This post should be titled "Reaction" and is due at the end of the online week.

6. *Debrief.* All students then write a second reply to their original thread with a reflection on the protocol itself. They title these "Debrief." This posting is due at the same time as the "Reaction" posting.

Variation

This protocol can also be used in blended formats with steps 5 and 6 done synchronously.

CHAPTER 7

Jumping into the Future

When we authors still had little more than a tentative title for this chapter, Beth and Joe turned on their car radio on the way to closing day at the organic farm stand. They happened to hit Terry Gross, several minutes into one of her *Fresh Air* interviews on National Public Radio. They had missed the introduction of her interviewee, but perked up when Gross asked him to imagine what the Web is becoming rather than what it already is. Her question seemed to ask him to *jump into the future*—the chapter's tentative title, and an echo of "Jumping In," the final chapter title of *The Power of Protocols*. Joe and Beth were deeply disappointed, however, by the interviewee's response. He merely described, in a very pedestrian manner, a trend toward interactive rather than passive web pages. The Web will be increasingly used, he said, for trading in information as well as in goods and services. "Already," he added, "when I want to find out the movies playing in Silicon Valley, I just go on the Web instead of looking them up in the newspaper or calling the theaters." At this point, Joe and Beth exchanged a look meant to ask, "Why in the world is Terry Gross talking with this guy?"

By the time they pulled into the farm stand, however, they had learned that the interviewee was Apple founder Steve Jobs who had recently died and that the interview had first aired in 1996 (Gross, 1996). As it turns out, the future one manages to hit when one jumps toward it—no matter how brilliant one is, or how hard one tries—turns pretty quickly to past. Yet there seems to be great value in the jumping. It forces us to anticipate change and, in retrospect especially, helps us appreciate the great pace of it.

Thus at the next online authors' meeting following their time-traveling ride to the organic market with Steve Jobs, Joe and Beth proposed ending this book with a little jumping contest. And Janet and Alan agreed. We asked some protocol-savvy friends to dream up an online protocol—to jump into the future, though not in huge leaps (as if many of us can even imagine huge leaps). We asked for little leaps instead that might stimulate our readers' sense of adventure. We got lots of rough ideas back, for example, about exploiting dramatically the video-making capacities of the Web (Steve Goodman), about an online museum of student work and protocols for visiting it (Ron Berger and Steve Seidel), and about using crowdsourcing as a teaching tool (Steven Strull).[1] And within the limits of the little time we gave them, a greater number of our friends than we had any right to expect came through with actual protocol sketches. We include three of these below—ones we single out for certain special qualities we mention. Of course, in a couple of years or less, these protocol jumpers will sound like the 1996 Steve Jobs did in October 2011, but we prize how they sound now. We hope their voices will inspire our readers to take a jump into the future too, and we end the book with some tips for jumping.

ASK THREE, THEN ME

The first protocol, Ask Three, Then Me, is a simple but bold one from Anne Burgunder, NYU professor and math education consultant. The simplicity derives from the protocol's roots in early elementary classrooms and the boldness from its brave trust in social networking.

When she works with teachers on implementing the Common Core Standards, Anne told us, the first student tasks they create often seem "off"—distortions in some fashion of the intentions underlying the standards. In the protocol she imagines, Anne would deal with this problem by taking advantage of the growing number of bloggers and social media networks for mathematics teachers. She would say to the teachers and prospective teachers she works with (adapting a phrase some of them use powerfully with their own students): "Ask three, before you ask me." And she would point them to the Internet and to the bloggers and networkers who inhabit it.

Thus a teacher participant in this protocol, after composing a task that he or she thinks jibes well with the Common Core, posts it to a small group of others (selected after a Web search of blogging/networking math educators). It is not necessary to know these others personally. The author of the task simply emails the task and asks, "Do you think this task embeds content or a practice called for by the Common Core?" The post asks potential responders to explain their answers and in the process point to wording from the standards.

Three people would have to respond with agree/disagree statements using direct references from the Common Core, before the person who has posted can respond. Once the "ask three" requirement has been met, the person who posted synthesizes the responses for the benefit of all who responded and announces his or her choice among two possible next steps:

- Keep the original task along with a clear rationale and citations to actual wording from the Common Core Standards, and start using it with students.
- Abandon the task with a rationale for why it does not meet the practices and/or content of the Common Core—again with citations to wording from the standards.

The outcome of this protocol, Anne thinks, would be to deepen the knowledge and practices of at least four mathematics educators and, perhaps, to lend to them and others a continuing source of social learning and support.

DESCRIBE, RESPOND, ACT

The next jumping-into-the-future protocol is Miriam Raider-Roth's Describe, Respond, Act. She is a professor of Educational Studies at the University of Cincinnati and has worked extensively with teachers using Descriptive Processes (Carini, 2001). The protocol she imagines supports university students who are mentoring middle school students in Place Out of Time, an online simulation game developed by the Interactive Communications and Simulations group at the University of Michigan. We especially like this protocol for its teaching-within-gaming design.

Each participant in the Place Out of Time simulation assumes a character (historical or contemporary) who might have something to say about a scenario from another time. Imagine Galileo, Emma Goldman, Nelson Mandela, and Evita Perón discussing whether a U.S. National Reservist who has served two tours of duty in Afghanistan and is a single mother should have to serve a third tour. The learning goals of Place Out of Time with respect to the middle school players include historical, ethical, and critical thinking via play, imagination, and theatricality. At the same time, the mentors who support the middle school students are learning how to identify and act on opportunities for supporting, challenging, and extending the students' learning. And here, again, the means are play, imagination, and theatricality.

While the original support seminars for mentors of the Place Out of Time simulation were face-to-face ones, Miriam has designed an online seminar and imagines a protocol that can help mentors learn to see the middle school students' learning more clearly. The protocol asks the mentors to describe what their mentees are saying, work collaboratively to understand the learning opportunities in the mentees' work and then to take intelligent action (Dewey, 1933; Rodgers, 2006) to support their learning. Here are Miriam's proposed protocol steps:

1. *Describe a puzzling post.* Choose a mentee's post that puzzles you— one that genuinely confuses, surprises, or catches you off-guard. Post the original puzzling post, plus a description of it, sentence by sentence. For practice in describing, think about how you might paraphrase (or say in your own words) the following post. It was composed by a mentee playing Anne Frank in dialogue with a mentor playing Queen Isabella of Spain: "Have you ever thought that people wanted a say in what they did with their own lives? Have you ever thought that maybe you're not a very good leader? Have you ever thought about the word 'good'? Who says what a good leader is?"

2. *Respond to two descriptions.* Once all other mentors have posted, respond to two. Read the original posts carefully, as well as the descriptions, and respond with an analysis of the opportunities these posts seem to present in supporting the mentees' historical, ethical, and/or critical thinking. Stretch your imagination and consider the improvisational, theatrical, and play opportunities that the students' posts offer.

3. *Take action.* After reading all of the responses to your description, tell the whole group what action you plan to take and your reason for doing so.

THE REPLAY/RESOURCE/REHEARSE PROTOCOL

Our final jumping-into-the-future protocol is from David Allen, a professor of education at the College of Staten Island and author of several books about protocols. We love this one for its intellectual ambition and for its unusually expansive embrace of Web 2.0 tools.

This protocol's purpose is to foster John Dewey's (1897) famous conception of education as the "continuing reconstruction of experience." It builds on other protocols, especially the Consultancy protocol and Success Analysis Protocol, to support participants in learning from reflection on experience. To do so, it introduces practices from theater artists, including Augusto Boal (1979), Anna Halprin (1995), Anne Bogart (Bogart & Landau, 2005), and others, who have developed processes for collaborative creation of new work for performance (plays, dance, etc.). Finally, it borrows from the work of Ilana Horn (2010), who has identified the role of *replays* and *instructional rehearsals* as key conceptual resources in teachers' learning discussions.

The protocol can be done synchronously or asynchronously but will probably work best as a hybrid, as noted in the steps below. It needs a facilitator with knowledge of online tools as well as protocols.

Steps

1. *Replay.* In this step, the presenter recounts a personal experience (from the classroom or elsewhere) that he or she would like to reconstruct, that is, open up for multiple interpretations. To do so, he or she can use written narrative, artifacts, video, or any other representational mode that is helpful and that available technology supports. He or she can also include a focus question or problem for participants.
2. *Clarify.* Here participants ask clarifying questions and the presenter addresses these as accurately and concisely as possible.
3. *Resource* (as a verb). Next, participants, either as individuals or in teams, seek out and post resources they believe might support or provoke the presenter in reconstructing his or her experience. They think expansively about resource types! These might include links to articles, images, videos (on YouTube or Vimeo), websites, personal narratives, and other resources. This step probably requires hours or days, and should include a deadline for posting.
4. *Explore resources.* The presenter reviews the resources posted and reflects on how these relate to or illuminate the initial experience recounted.

5. *Rehearse.* The presenter provides a *reconstructed* version of the initial experience. How might it have been different if the presenter had exploited some of the resources posted? What might the presenter have done differently? What might he or she do in similar situations to come? The presenter uses any mode of representation the technology supports to depict the reconstruction: oral or written narrative, schematic or graphic representation, etc.

6. *Reflect.* All participants reflect on the rehearsal: How has it reconstructed the initial experience? What new questions, possibilities, or problems does it open up? The facilitator plays a key role here in opening up the discussion and involving all participants.

7. *Reflect on process.* To what extent has this protocol achieved or not its goal of advancing learning by reconstructing experience? How would participants tweak or revise it for the next time?

ADVICE TO JUMPERS

Clearly, our jumping-into-the-future contestants whose protocols we sketch above made their jumps with passionate interests in mind—ones related to their work as adventurous educators. So our first piece of advice to you as potential jumpers is to find your own comparably passionate interest. Is it about solving a chronic teaching and learning problem, as Anne's seems to be; taking an existing course online as Miriam's is (and as lots of jumps described in this book have been); or dreaming big about Web 2.0 tools and learning, as David's surely is? Our second piece of advice is to name the risk you feel in jumping (which is also the opportunity you are seizing). Is it about the technology, the protocol, the teaching online, or some combination of these? Every jumper defines *future* in a different way with respect to the matters taken up in this book, but naming it lends focus to the jump. It will also help you navigate our mix-and-match lists of advice below.

Ways to Get Started with Protocols

- Pick a simple protocol that doesn't have many steps. Try it out with people you feel comfortable with and debrief the experience to figure out what worked and what didn't.

- Stick with the steps provided in the protocol before adapting them.
- Now try it out with students. Let them in on the trial run—to elicit both their suspension of disbelief up front and their good faith feedback at the end.
- Observe others facilitating protocols using different media and for different purposes.
- Consider learning more, for example, by exploring some of the books and websites mentioned in this book and by creating or joining a professional learning community or critical friends group that regularly uses protocols. The annual winter meeting of the School Reform Initiative is a good place to find or form such a group—whether a face-to-face one or an online one.

Ways to Get Started with Web 2.0 Teaching

- Experiment with a small-group assignment that you are used to asking your students to do face-to-face. Ask the groups to work online instead, on a platform of their choice. Chances are they are familiar with Facebook, maybe other platforms also. Plain email may be okay too. Just ask them to document their work in a way that can be attached to or embedded in an email message they send you at the end of the week—say, the transcript of a conversation, a folder of photos, a document they wrote jointly, a set of websites they bookmarked. Let them sort out all the details, not only the platform, but the deadlines, the timelines, who posts, etc. But tell them they must be prepared to share these details with you and others in class.
- Do the above again, but this time, tell the students to use a protocol you found in this book and that seems appropriate for the assignment.
- Take advantage of workshops or classes to learn new technologies for teaching.
- Form a support group of colleagues willing to experiment with using protocols in new media.
- Learn to laugh when technology doesn't work the way you had planned.
- Observe others facilitating with technologies that are new to you before you try them yourself.
- When you do try them, talk a friend into being your co-facilitator, with one of you minding the group and the other the technology.

Ways to Go Online with Protocols Once You Have the Basics Down

- Look for protocols that serve your purpose. Are you discussing texts? Solving a problem? Trying to understand your students better? Protocols are generally organized around these themes. In addition to the protocols described in this book, you'll find many protocols organized by purpose in *The Power of Protocols* (McDonald et al., 2007) and at the website of the School Reform Initiative (http://www.schoolreforminitiative.org).
- Look for protocols that have just a few steps. Protocols with lots of steps are harder to implement in online environments. Bear in mind that steps take longer in online environments. Try to consolidate or eliminate some.
- Figure out how long each step should take and, for asynchronous environments, what deadlines to give participants to complete the steps.
- Remember that you cannot just tell people what to discuss and when; you must also specify where. For asynchronous discussions, you need to provide a discussion forum or thread. For synchronous discussions, you need to provide a link or a virtual meeting space.
- Double-check directions to make sure they are very specific and detailed; otherwise, participants may get confused and not know what to do.
- Think about how the protocol will look on the platform you've chosen. For example, consider directing students to give posts meaningful titles to enhance readability, especially when using threaded discussion forums.
- Plan blended protocols based on what works best in real time (for example, a discussion meant to energize the group) and what works best in asynchronous blocks (for example, time to compose or search or react to complex input).

Things That Make It Easier

- Spend additional time up front having everyone get to know one another and building trust. It takes longer to build trust in online environments, so allot more time than you would with a face-to-face setting.

- Take the time to establish norms for participation. How frequently should everyone check in with the teacher in asynchronous settings? How much before a synchronous meeting should students arrive to troubleshoot technology issues? Make sure one of the norms encourages risk taking, and let everyone know that you expect and forgive mistakes.
- Give students time to explore synchronous environments before getting started. Encourage them also to change their avatars or photos, use emoticons, and experiment with other available features. Give everyone permission to play and have fun.
- Always provide a way for students to ask questions. In asynchronous formats, you can provide a Questions forum where everyone can see the answers. For synchronous formats, provide a phone number at which you can be reached.
- Email directions to students ahead of time so that they know what to expect. And, for synchronous formats, ask students to print out the directions so they can keep them handy.
- Provide models or examples for students to follow of what you are looking for.
- Send reminders of deadlines to keep everyone on track, and email individuals who forget. Knowing that the teacher is present and aware of when students are not contributing can keep them involved.
- Publicly acknowledge students who contribute in ways you would like others to emulate, but do it subtly so as to avoid embarrassing them or others.
- Wherever possible, share facilitation—one facilitator to focus on technology troubleshooting and one to focus on the process and content of the discussion. Or ask your students to act as facilitators of small groups. This is particularly helpful for larger classes.
- Have a backup plan—one that leaves room for technology glitches.
- Most importantly, find the courage to educate yourself, try new things, explore new territory, take risks.

One, two, three . . . *jump.*

Notes

Chapter 1

1. The Tuning Protocol was developed by Joe McDonald and colleagues at the Coalition of Essential Schools; the Consultancy protocol was developed by Gene Thompson-Grove and colleagues at the Annenberg Institute for School Reform; and the Collaborative Assessment Conference was developed by Steve Seidel and colleagues at Harvard Project Zero. Step-by-step descriptions of these and many other protocols can be found in McDonald, Mohr, Dichter, & McDonald (2003, 2007); Easton (2009); and the online collection of the School Reform Initiative at www.schoolreforminitiative.org.

2. See City, Elmore, Fiarman, & Teitel (2009) for a full description of this and several other protocols.

3. What Comes Up? was created by Simon Clements. See McDonald, Mohr, Dichter, & McDonald (2007).

4. Standard usage is still emerging with regard to whether to call a mix of online and face-to-face teaching *blended* or *hybrid* (Snart, 2010). However, we follow the Sloane Foundation (which has tracked the phenomenon) and also the Library of Congress in using the word *blended* exclusively.

5. The phrase Web 2.0 refers to the fact that the Web is increasingly used today not just to read and download other people's content, but to create content—as, for example, a user does when he or she posts a video to YouTube, shares pictures on a social networking site like Facebook, or blogs to the world about his or her visit to Atlantic City or Patagonia.

6. Underlining the controversies embedded in what we call above the new constitutional arrangements, a recent front-page article in the *New York Times* (Saul, 2011) singled out K12 Inc. for criticism, describing it as "a company that tries to squeeze profits from public school dollars by raising enrollment, increasing teacher workload and lowering standards" (p. A1/A24).

7. Hypertext is highlighted text on a computer that embeds a hyperlink. Readers who click on it access a related web-based text.

8. A *bookmark* in Web parlance is what you create when you add a particular website to your list of favorites in your online browser. *Social bookmarking* is what you do when you go to a social bookmarking site—for example, the site called Delicious (aptly named for the analogy we are drawing here). Such sites are designed for people to share their bookmarks with each other, and to form interest groups—for example, around using protocols in online teaching. Such groups can be powerful inquiry and learning groups, and make substantial contributions to a field.

9. We think especially of the School Reform Initiative (http://www.schoolreforminitiative. org).

10. Chatting involves a synchronous exchange on the computer among two or more people. Adobe Connect, a video conferencing tool, provides users the opportunity to chat by typing.

11. Skype is an Internet-based software application currently owned by Microsoft. It allows users (whether calling point to point or conferencing) to communicate with each other by voice, video, and/or instant messaging.

12. After the 1991 Gus Van Sant film with its soundtrack song by the B-52s.

Chapter 2

1. Key among them were Professor Rosa Pietanza who is the main course instructor today and Professor Joe McDonald who co-teaches with her. Others who assisted include Professor James Fraser, and staff from the New York City Department of Education, especially Amy McIntosh and Audra Watson. The overall director of the effort was Professor Alyson Taub who supported the use of protocols and advocated taking the course online.

2. For a complete description of Gallery Walk steps, see the School Reform Initiative's extensive archive of protocols at http://www.schoolreforminitiative.org.

3. This variation of the Panel Protocol was inspired by Kathleen Cushman's books. See, for example, Cushman & Students from What Kids Can Do (2005, 2010).

4. Facebook is a social networking tool. Users can upload pictures, share news, message, and chat with one another. They can keep pages private (for their Facebook friends only) or allow access to any Facebook users. Google Docs is a free web-based suite of tools that enable the collaborative creation of online texts. Google Talk is an Internet-based software application that enables users to chat with voice and video, either person to person or between groups, and on desktops or hand-held computers.

5. The restructurers themselves were often quick to point out that they were as much interested in school cultures as in school structures.

6. The Coalition of Essential Schools (Tuning Protocol) and the teacher communities created by the various research activities of Harvard Project Zero (the Collaborative Assessment Conference).

7. The Standards in Practice Protocol was developed by Education Trust. See McDonald et al. (2007) for a description of the protocol.

8. For more information about Socratic or seminar pedagogy, see Adler (1982), and the National Paideia Center (2011). For insights about games pedagogy, see Gee (2007). For insights about case study pedagogy, see Barnes, Christensen, and Hansen (1994) and Christensen, Garvin, and Sweet (1992). For insights into service learning pedagogy, see Youniss and Levine (2009) or the National Youth leadership Council (http://www.nylc.org/) For more information on what we're calling project-and-expedition pedagogy, see Berger (2003), Crawford (2009), and Expeditionary Learning Schools (www.elschools.org). Workshop pedagogy has many sources. In literacy, see Calkins and Harwayne (1987); more generally, see Crawford (2009). Finally, for information about what we're calling Doug Lemov pedagogy, see Lemov (2010), Merseth (2009), and Green (2010).

9. All of the protocols we've highlighted so far in the book involve text making and text reading. Other notable ones that also involve text making and text reading include the Final

Word Protocol, the Success Analysis Protocol, the Shadow Protocol, and the Minnesota Slice (See McDonald et al., 2007). They also include Chalk Talk and Gap Analysis Protocol (see the School Reform Initiative archive of protocols at www.schoolreforminitiative.org).

10. See the New York State Peer Review Protocol in the 2003 edition of *The Power of Protocols* or the Peer Review Protocol, to be featured in the forthcoming third edition of that book.

11. The first three of these protocols are described in McDonald et al. (2007) and the other two at the website of the School Reform Initiative (http://www.schoolreforminitiative.org).

12. Asynchronous discussions are those in which discussants post and review messages at different times over a defined period of time. Synchronous discussions are real-time discussions—for example, by means of typing in chat boxes, or using a voice tool (with or without video) like Skype or Google Talk.

13. See a description of Save the Last Word for Me in Chapter 3. It is a variation of the Final Word Protocol, described step by step in McDonald et al. (2007).

Chapter 3

1. Wang and Gearhart (2006) define a course management system as "a Web server software application package that provides an integrated online environment for administration of student enrollment, course setup, content creation and organization, online communication, online assessment, and student performance monitoring" (p. 287). Another term in use is content management system. Blackboard and WebCT (now owned by Blackboard, originally its competitor) are examples of course management systems. Some universities and other online education providers use learning management systems (LMSs) rather than course management systems, or the umbrella term virtual learning environments. LMSs afford students opportunities to manage (including time manage) multiple courses and other activities. Some learning management systems—notably Sakai and Moodle—are open-source systems. The term *open source* means that users have access to the computer code on which the software is based and can legally make and share modifications. Thus, for example, the University of Rhode Island (URI) can create a unique Sakai platform, and the University of North Carolina at Chapel Hill can borrow some of the URI features.

2. David Cohen (2011) makes a useful distinction between inattentive teaching, which is the source of much of what we learn in life, and attentive teaching, which is what concerns us in this book. The attentive teacher gives deliberate attention to learning—including what is to be learned, how it is to be learned, and whether it is ever learned. This is another way to describe what we call the "deal." But a student gets most of the cues about the teacher's attentiveness or awareness of the deal (and thus to some extent the chances of actually learning) from the teacher's presence—does he or she seem attentive? And presence is easier to achieve in face-to face environments than in online ones.

3. A threaded discussion is a common feature of many Internet "discussion boards." Each topic within the discussion board is a new forum, and threads are subtopics. Participants can initiate new threads at will, or post a reply to an existing thread.

4. For additional details of this experience, see Zydney, deNoyelles, and Seo (2012).

5. The Making Meaning Protocol: The Storytelling Version was created by Daniel Baron.

See the School Reform Initiative's online collection of protocols at www.schoolreforminitia-tive.org for the usual steps involved.

6. Save the Last Word for Me is an adaptation of the Final Word protocol described in McDonald et al. (2007).

7. For additional details on this protocol, see Chapter 5.

8. For a glance at School of One, see YouTube (http://www.youtube.com/watch?v-=HSTrI6nj5xU). For more about the platoon system, devised by Gary, Indiana, superin-tendent of schools William Wirt, see Tyack (1974) and also http://en.wikipedia.org/wiki/William_Wirt_(educator).

9. An intranet is a private network for a particular organization. Its pages look like web pages, but access to them is restricted.

10. For an in-depth account of Hull's and her colleagues' semiotic methods, see Hull and Nelson (2005). For the steps of Peeling the Onion protocol and other text-rendering proto-cols, see McDonald et al. (2007) and also the School Reform Initiative archive of protocols at http://www,schoolreforminitiative.org.

11. iMovie is a video-editing software application used on Macintosh computers.

12. For a full description of the Cosmopolitan Protocol, see McDonald et al., 2007).

13. Bandwidth is a measure of the rate of data transfer over the internet or network.

14. Khan Academy is an inventive, self-paced virtual learning environment that features over 3,000 short instructional videos, as well as other learning resources, mostly in math and science (www.khanacademy.org) .

15. Google Docs and Dropbox are both free tools (up to a certain limit of capacity) that allow users to store and share documents and access them from any computer. Google Docs also features document production tools for presentations, spreadsheets, survey forms, and so on.

16. Second Life is an online virtual world, created by Linden Lab in 2003, by which users create places and objects, including avatars (which may or may not resemble themselves) who explore these and other spaces and interact with other avatars they encounter there. Users also can buy and sell goods and services. See http://www.secondlife.com. Video tu-torials to learn how to use the environment are located at http://wiki.secondlife.com/wiki/Video_Tutorials#Official_Video_Tutorials. According to Wikipedia, Second Life had one million active users in 2011. See http://en.wikipedia.org/wiki/Second_Life, and also http://secondlife.com/whatis/?lang=en-US.

17. For a description of the Common Core Standards in literacy and mathematics, pro-mulgated by the Council of Chief State School Officers and the National Governors Asso-ciation and now adopted by most states, see http://www.corestandards.org/.

Chapter 4

1. See McDonald et al. (2007) for a fuller description of Marvin's Model. This protocol is often used to preview the content of an individual lesson as well as a whole course.

2. Prezi is a zooming presentation editor that enables easy collaboration among authors; Animoto is a video slideshow maker with music; Photopeach is a slideshow maker; and VoiceThread enables group conversation around an image, document, presentation, etc.

3. Ning is an online platform that enables organizations to operate a customized website

with Web 2.0 production capacities to create and share photos, videos, discussion forums, and blogs. It is owned by Glam Media.

4. Edmodo is a free social learning network for teachers and students.

Chapter 5

1. The GoingOn Academic Engagement Network describes its platform—designed specifically for colleges and universities—as "an academic social network where students and faculty can create and participate in online communities, collaborate using live Facebook-like activity streams, and curate their academic network—while keeping it all separate from their personal social networks" (http://www.goingon.com/goingon-platform)

2. As a guide to teaching with Start, Steer, Summarize, NTC uses a rubric developed by Peggy Taylor, director of the Masters of Science in Science Education (MSSE) program at Montana State University. The rubric is used to assess a facilitator's practice with respect to content, focus, community, and reflection.

3. The Common Core Standards for mathematics (see note 17 in Chapter 3) are constructed on the basis of a set of recommended core teaching practices. In this example, Anne Burgunder is not only teaching problem solving (the factoring problem) but also the core practices.

Chapter 6

1. See a description of the face-to-face Charrette Protocol at http://schoolreforminitiative.org/protocol/doc/charrette.pdf.

2. Other members of the regular instructional team include Rosa Pietanza, Fred Kaeser, Cliff Cohen, Renae Despointes, Rosa Casiello O'Day, Pat Romandetto, and Beth McDonald.

3. Google Docs is a free web-based suite of tools that enable online collaboration. Social Responsibility students who opt to use Google Docs create and modify over a specified period of time a word processing document that records their various contributions in the form of a script (for example, "Dan: I think that Aptheker is saying . . . ; Kai: I'm not sure I agree . . . ; etc.") Podcasts are digital audio recordings—in this case, of a group using a single device like a handheld computer—that are uploaded to the course server. Community podcasts are web-based recording sessions with voice input from different computers. E-chat is a keyboard-based conversation in real time. Instead of talking, participants type.

4. See McDonald et al., 2007.

5. See the SRI website (http://www.schoolreforminitiative.org) or McDonald et al. (2007) for the face-to-face version of this protocol.

Chapter 7

1. Crowdsourcing is open problem solving wherein problems—for example, design problems—are outsourced to all Web users who care to respond to a prompt, and participants form an online community to select the best solutions.

References

Adler, M. (1982). *The Paideia proposal: An educational manifesto*. New York: Collier Books.

Allen, D. (Ed.). (1998). *Assessing student learning: From grading to understanding*. New York: Teachers College Press.

Allen, D., & Blythe, T. (2004). *The facilitator's book of questions: Tools for looking together at student and teacher work*. New York: Teachers College Press.

Allen, I. E., & Seaman, J. (2011). *Going the distance: Online education in the United States, 2011*. The Sloan Consortium. Retrieved from http://sloanconsortium.org/publications/survey/going_distance_2011

Appiah, K. A. (2006). *Cosmopolitanism: Ethics in a world of strangers*. New York: Norton.

Baran, E., & Correia, A. (2009). Student-led facilitation strategies in online discussions. *Distance Education, 30*, 339–361.

Barnes, L. B., Christensen, C. R., & Hansen, A. (1994). *Teaching and the case method*. Boston: Harvard Business School Press.

Beach, R., Hull, G. A., & O'Brien, D. (2011). Transforming English language arts in a Web 2.0 world. In D. Lapp and D. Fisher (Eds.), *Handbook of research on teaching the English language arts* (3rd ed., pp. 161–167). New York: Routledge.

Berger, R. (2003). *Ethic of excellence: Building a culture of craftsmanship with students*. Portsmouth, NH: Heinemann.

Boal, A. (1979). *Theatre of the oppressed*. London: Pluto Press.

Bogart, A., & Landau, T. (2005). *The viewpoints book: A practical guide to viewpoints and composition*. New York: Theatre Communications Group.

Boudett, K. P., City, E. A., & Murnane, R. J. (2005). *Data wise*. Cambridge, MA: Harvard Education Press.

Bransford, J. D., Brown, A. L., & Cocking, R. R. (2000). *How people learn: Brain, mind, experience, and school*. Washington, DC: National Academy Press.

Brown, J. S., & Duguid, P. (2000). *The social life of information*. Boston: Harvard Business School Press.

Calkins, L. M., & Harwayne, S. (1987). *The writing workshop: A world of difference*. Portsmouth, NH: Heinemann.

Carini, P. F. (2001). *Starting strong: A different look at children, schools, and standards*. New York, NY: Teachers College Press.

Chen, M. (2010). *Education nation: Six leading edges of innovation in our schools*. San Francisco: Jossey-Bass.

Christensen, C. R., Garvin, D. A., & Sweet, A. (1992). *Education for judgment*. Boston: Harvard Business School Press.

City, E. A., Elmore, R. F., Fiarman, S. E., & Teitel, L. (2009). *Instructional rounds in education: A network approach to improving teaching and learning.* Cambridge, MA: Harvard Education Press.

Clark, R. E. (2009). How much and what type of guidance is optimal for learning from instruction? In S. Tobias & T. M. Duffy (Eds.), *Constructivist instruction: Success or failure?* (pp. 158–183). New York: Taylor & Francis.

Cohen, D. K. (2011). *Teaching and its predicaments.* Cambridge, MA: Harvard University Press.

Collins, A., Joseph, D., & Bielaczyc, K. (2004). Design research: Theoretical and methodological issues. *Journal of the Learning Sciences, 13*(1), 15–42.

Conole, G., & Oliver, M. (Eds.) (2007). *Contemporary perspectives in e-learning research.* New York: Routledge.

Crawford, M. B. (2009). *Shop class as soulcraft: An inquiry into the value of work.* New York: Penguin.

Curry, M. W. (2008). Critical friends groups: The possibilities and limitations embedded in teacher professional communities aimed at instructional improvement and school reform. *Teachers College Record, 110*(4), 733–774.

Cushman, K., & Students from What Kids Can Do. (2005). *Fires in the bathroom: Advice for teachers from high school students.* New York: New Press.

Cushman, K., & Students from What Kids Can Do. (2010). *Fires in the mind: What kids can tell us about motivation and mastery.* San Francisco: Jossey-Bass.

Darling-Hammond, L., Ancess, J., & Falk, B. (1995). *Authentic assessment in action: Studies of schools and students at work.* New York: Teachers College Press.

Darling-Hammond, L., & Sykes, G. (1999). *Teaching as the learning profession: Handbook of policy and practice.* San Francisco: Jossey-Bass.

Del Prete, T. (2010). *Improving the odds: Developing powerful teaching practice and a culture of learning in urban high schools.* New York: Teachers College Press.

Deming, W. E. (1986). *Out of crisis.* Cambridge, MA: Center for Advanced Engineering Study.

Dewey, J. (1897). My pedagogic creed. *School Journal, 54*(January), 77–80.

Dewey, J. (1933). *How we think.* Boston, MA: Heath. (Original published in 1910).

DuFour, R., DuFour, R., Eaker, R., & Many, T. (2010). *Learning by doing: A handbook for professional communities at work* (2nd ed.). Bloomington, IN: Solution Tree Press.

Dweck, C. S. (1999). *Self-theories: Their role in motivation, personality, and development.* Philadelphia: Psychology Press.

Eagleton, T. (1983). *Literary theory.* Oxford, United Kingdom: Blackwell.

Easton, L. B. (2009). *Protocols for professional learning.* Alexandria, VA: ASCD.

Elbow, P. (1986). *Embracing contraries: Explorations in learning and teaching.* New York: Oxford University Press.

Garrison, D. R., Anderson, T., & Archer, W. (2001). Critical thinking, cognitive presence, and computer conferencing in distance education. *American Journal of Distance Education, 15*(1): 7–23.

Garrison, D. R., & Anderson, T. (2003). *E-learning in the 21st century: A framework for research and practice.* New York: RoutledgeFalmer.

Gee, J. P. (2007). *What videogames have to teach us about learning and literacy.* New York: Palgrave Macmillan.

Gilbert, P. K., & Dabbagh, N. (2005). How to structure online discussions for meaningful discourse: A case study. *British Journal of Educational Technology, 36*, 5–18.

Green, E. (2010, March 2). Building a better teacher. *New York Times*. Retrieved from http://www.nytimes.com/2010/03/07/magazine/07Teachers-t.html

Gross, T. (1996). Interview with Steve Jobs, *Fresh Air*. Rebroadcast on National Public Radio, October 25, 2011. Retrieved from http://www.npr.org/player/v2/mediaPlayer.html?action=1&t=1&islist=false&id=141653658&m=141122790

Guralnick, D., & Larson, D. (2009). The cultural impact of e-learning and intranets on corporate employees. In S. Wheeler (Ed.), *Connected minds, emerging cultures: Cybercultures in online learning* (pp. 247–260). Charlotte, NC: Information Age.

Halprin, A. (1995). *Moving towards life: Five decades of transformation dance* (R. Kaplan, Ed.). Middletown, CT: Wesleyan University Press.

Hamilton, E., & Cherniavsky, J. (2006). Issues in synchronous versus asynchronous e-learning platforms. In H. F. O'Neil & R. S. Perez (Eds.), *Web-based learning: Theory, research, and practice* (pp. 87–106). Mahwah, NJ: Lawrence Erlbaum.

Hansen, D. T. (2010). Cosmopolitanism and education: A view from the ground. *Teachers College Record, 112*(1), 1–30.

Herrington, J., Reeves, T. C., & Oliver, R. (2010). *A guide to authentic e-learning*. New York: Routledge.

Himley, M. with Carini, P. F. (2000). *From another angle: Children's strengths and school standards*. New York: Teachers College Press.

Holtzapple, E. (2001). *Standards in Practice: Year one evaluation*. Cincinnati, OH: Cincinnati Public Schools.

Horn, I. S. (2010). Teaching replays, teaching rehearsals, and re-visions of practice: Learning from colleagues in a mathematics teacher community. *Teachers College Record, 112*(1), 225–259.

Hull, G. A., Kenney, N. L., Marple, S., & Forsman-Schneider, A. (2006). Many versions of masculine. *Afterschool matters* (Occasional paper series). New York: Robert Bowne Foundation. Retrieved from http://www.bownefoundation.org/pdf_files/occasional_paper_05.pdf

Hull, G. A., & Nelson, M. E. (2005). Locating the semiotic power of multimodality. *Written Communication, 22*(2), 224–261.

Hull, G. A., & Stornaiuolo, A. (2010). Literate arts in a global world: Reframing social networking as cosmopolitan practice. *Journal of Adolescent & Adult Literacy, 54*(2), 85–97.

Hull, G. A., Stornaiuolo, A., & Sahni, U. (2010). Cultural citizenship and cosmopolitan practice: Global youth communicate online. *English Education, 42*(4, July), 331–367.

Jonassen, D. H. (1991). Objectivism versus constructivism: Do we need a new philosophical paradigm? *Educational Technology Research and Development, 39*(3), 5–14.

Jones, C., Cook, J., Jones, A., & de Laat, M. (2007). Collaboration. In G. Conole & M. Oliver (Eds.), *Contemporary perspectives in e-learning research* (pp. 174–189). New York: Routledge.

K12. (2011). *Corporate profile*. Retrieved from http://investors.k12.com/phoenix.zhtml?c=214389&p=irol-homeProfile&t=&id=&

Kamenetz, A. (2010). *DIY U: Edupunks, edupreneurs, and the coming transformation of higher education*. White River Junction, VT: Chelsea Green.

Keller, B. (2011, October 3). The university of wherever. *New York Times*, p. A25.

Kirschner, P. A. (2009). Epistemology or pedagogy, that is the question. In S. Tobias & T.M. Duffy (Eds.), *Constructivist instruction: Success or failure?* (pp. 144–157). New York: Taylor & Francis.

Lehman, R. M., & Berg, R. A. (2007). *147 practical tips for synchronous and blended technology teaching and learning.* Madison, WI: Atwood.

Lehman, R. M., & Conçeicão, S. C. O. (2010). *Creating a sense of presence in online teaching.* San Francisco: Jossey-Bass.

Lemov, D. (2010). *Teach like a champion: 49 techniques that put students on the path to college.* San Francisco: Jossey-Bass.

Lewin, T. (2011, August 25). Online enterprises gain foothold as path to a college degree. *New York Times.* Retrieved from http://www.nytimes.com/2011/08/25/education/25future.html?scp=3&sq=higher%20education&st=cse

Little, J. W., Gearhart, M., Curry, M., & Kafka, J. (2003). Looking at student work for teacher learning, teacher community, and school reform. *Phi Delta Kappan, 83*(3), 185–192.

Louis, K. S., & Marks, H. M. (1998). Does professional learning community affect the classroom? Teachers' work and student experiences in restructuring school. *American Journal of Education, 106*(4), 532–575.

Markoff, J. (2012). Online education venture lures cash infusion and deals with 5 top universities. *New York Times.* Retrieved from http://www.nytimes.com/2012/04/18/technology/coursera-plans-to-announce-university-partners-for-online-classes.html

Maurino, P. S. M, Federman, F., & Greenwald, L. (2007–2008). Online threaded discussions: Purposes, goals, and objectives. *Journal of Educational Technology Systems, 36*, 129–143. doi: 10.2190/ET.36.2.b

McDonald, J. P. (1996). *Redesigning school: Lessons for the 21st century.* San Francisco: Jossey-Bass.

McDonald, J. P., & Hudder, D. (2012). *The deal.* Unpublished manuscript.

McDonald, J. P., Klein, E., & Riordan, M. (2009). *Going to scale with new school designs: Reinventing high school.* New York: Teachers College Press.

McDonald, J. P., Mohr, N., Dichter, A., & McDonald, E. C. (2003). *The power of protocols: An educator's guide to better practice.* New York: Teachers College Press.

McDonald, J. P., Mohr, N., Dichter, A., & McDonald, E. C. (2007). *The power of protocols: An educator's guide to better practice* (2nd ed.). New York: Teachers College Press.

McLaughlin, M. W., & Talbert, J. E. (2001). *Professional communities and the work of high school teaching.* Chicago: University of Chicago Press.

McLaughlin, M. W., & Talbert, J. E. (2006). *Building school-based teacher learning communities.* New York: Teachers College Press.

Merseth, K. M. (2009). *Inside urban charter schools.* Cambridge, MA: Harvard Education Press.

National Paideia Center. (2011). *About Paideia: Teaching practices.* National Paideia Center website. Retrieved from http://www.paideia.org/about-paideia/teaching-practices/

Newmann, F. M. (1996). *Authentic achievement: Restructuring schools for intellectual quality.* San Francisco: Jossey-Bass.

Palloff, R. M., & Pratt, K. (2005). *Collaborating online: Learning together in community.* San Francisco: Jossey-Bass.

Palloff, R. M., & Pratt, K. (2011). *The excellent online instructor: Strategies for professional development.* San Francisco: Jossey-Bass.

Papert, S. (1997). Why school reform is impossible. *Journal of the Learning Sciences, 6*(4), 417–427.

Phillips, J. (2003). Powerful learning: Creating learning communities in urban school reform. *Journal of Curriculum and Supervision, 18*(3), 240–258.

Plass, J. L., Homer, B. D., & Hayward, E. O. (2009). Design factors for educationally effective animations and simulations. *Journal of Computing in Higher Education, 21*, 31–61.

Powell, A., Farrar, E., & Cohen, D. K. (1985). *The shopping-mall high school: Winners and losers in the educational marketplace.* Boston: Houghton Mifflin.

Resnick, L. B. (1987). Learning in school and out. *Educational Researcher, 16*(9), 13–20.

Rodgers, C. (2006). Attending to student voice: The impact of descriptive feedback on learning and teaching. *Curriculum Inquiry, 36*(2), 209–237. doi: 0.1111/j.1467-873X.2006.00353.x

Saul, S. (2011, December 13). Profits and questions at online charter schools. *New York Times*, A1, A24–A25.

Scholes, R. (1983). *Semiotics and interpretation.* New Haven, CT: Yale University Press.

Scholes, R. (1985). *Textual power: Literary theory and the teaching of English.* New Haven, CT: Yale University Press.

Schwarz, A. (2011, October 18). Out with textbooks, in with laptops for an Indiana school district. *New York Times.* Retrieved from http://www.nytimes.com/2011/10/19/education/19textbooks.html?ref=education

Senge, P. (1990). *The fifth discipline: The art and practice of the learning organization.* New York: Doubleday.

Shulman, L. S. (2005). Signature pedagogies in the professions. *Daedalus, 134*(3), 52–59.

Siskin, L. S. (2011). Changing contexts and the challenge of high school reform in New York City. In J. A. O'Day, C. S. Bitter, & L. M. Gomez (Eds.), *Education reform in New York City* (pp. 181–198). Cambridge, MA: Harvard Education Press.

Snart, J. A. (2010). *Hybrid learning: The perils and promise of blending online and face-to-face instruction in higher education.* Santa Barbara, CA: Praeger.

Spiro R. J., Collins, B. P., Thota, J. J., & Feltovich, P. J. (2003). Cognitive flexibility theory: Hypermedia for complex learning, adaptive knowledge application, and experience acceleration. *Educational Technology, 45*(5), 5–10.

Spiro, R. J., Feltovich, P. J., Jacobson, M. J., & Coulson, R. L. (1991). Cognitive flexibility, constructivism, and hypertext: Random access instruction for advanced knowledge acquisition in ill-structured domains. *Education Technology, 31*(5), 24–33.

Stodel, E. J., Thompson, T. L., & MacDonald, C. J. (2006). Learners' perspectives on what is missing from online learning: Interpretations through the Community of Inquiry framework. *The International Review of Research in Open and Distance Learning, 7*(3). Retrieved from http://www.irrodl.org/index.php/irrodl/article/view/325/743

Streeter, B. H. (1931). *The chained library.* New York: Cambridge University Press.

Suarez-Orozco, M., & Suarez-Orozco, C. (2002). *Children of immigration.* Cambridge, MA: Harvard University Press.

Supovitz, J. A. (2002). Developing communities of instructional practice. *Teachers College Record, 104*(8), 1591–1626.

Supovitz, J. A., & Christman, J. B. (2003). *Developing communities of instructional practice: Lessons from Cincinnati and Philadelphia.* Philadelphia, PA: Consortium for Policy Research in Education, University of Pennsylvania.

Sweller, J. (2009). What human cognitive architecture tells us about constructivism. In S. Tobias & T. M. Duffy (Eds.), *Constructivist instruction: Success or failure?* (pp. 127–143). New York: Taylor & Francis.

Talbert, J. E. (2011). Collaborative inquiry to expand student success in New York City schools. In J. A. O'Day, C. S. Bitter, & L. M. Gomez (Eds.), *Education reform in New York City* (pp. 131–156). Cambridge, MA: Harvard Education Press.

Thomas, D., & Brown, J. S. (2011). *A new culture of learning: Cultivating the imagination for a world of constant change.* Lexington, KY: Author.

Thomas, M. J. W. (2002). Learning within incoherent structures: The space of online discussion forums. *Journal of Computer-Assisted Learning, 18*, 351–366.

Tobias, S., & Duffy, T. M. (Eds.). (2009). *Constructivist instruction: Success or failure?* New York: Routledge.

Tyack, D. B. (1974). *The one best system: A history of American urban education.* Cambridge, MA: Harvard University Press.

Tyack, D. B., & Cuban, L. (1995). *Tinkering toward utopia: A century of public school reform.* Cambridge, MA: Harvard University Press.

U. S. Departments of Commerce and Education & NetDay. (2004). *Visions: 2020.2—Student views on transforming education and training through advanced technologies.* Retrieved from http://www.tomorrow.org/speakup/pdfs/Visions2020-2.pdf

Vescio, V., Ross, D., & Adams, A. (2008). A review of research on the impact of professional learning communities on teaching practice and student learning. *Teaching and Teacher Education, 24*, 80–91.

Wang, H., & Gearhart, D. L. (2006). *Designing and developing web-based instruction.* Upper Saddle River, NJ: Pearson.

Wasley, P. A., Fine, M., Gladden, M., Holland, N. F., King, S. P., Mosak, E., & Powell, L. C. (2000). *Small schools, great strides: A study of new small schools in Chicago.* New York: Bank Street College of Education.

Wenger, E. (1998). *Communities of practice: Learning, meaning, and identity.* New York: Cambridge University Press.

Youniss, J., & Levine, P. (2009). *Engaging young people in civic life.* Nashville, TN: Vanderbilt University Press.

Zydney, J. M., deNoyelles, A., & Seo, K. K-J. (2012). Creating a community of inquiry in online environments: An exploratory study on the effect of a protocol on interactions within asynchronous environments. *Computers & Education, 58*(1), 77–87.

Index

About the Authors

Joseph P. McDonald is professor of Teaching and Learning at New York University's Steinhardt School of Culture, Education, and Human Development. He teaches in the English Education Program there and coordinates secondary teacher education. He also directs the Metro Learning Communities project at NYU's Metropolitan Center for Urban Education. McDonald previously taught at Brown University where he also served as a senior researcher for the Coalition of Essential Schools and director of research for the Annenberg Institute for School Reform. He has also been a middle- and high school English teacher, as well as a principal. He is the author or co-author of nine books about teaching and school reform, including *The Power of Protocols*, and *Going to Scale with New School Designs: Reinventing High School*. He lives in New York City and Wareham, Massachusetts, with his wife, Beth, and their West Highland terrier.

Janet Mannheimer Zydney is an associate professor in Curriculum & Instruction at University of Cincinnati's College of Education, Criminal Justice, and Human Services. She teaches classes in instruction design and technology and coordinates all sections of the undergraduate educational technology class for all pre-service teachers. Dr. Zydney's research is on the use of technology-based scaffolding in online environments, multimedia programs, and digital games for improving students' problem solving and critical thinking. She received her PhD in educational communication and technology in 2004 from New York University and completed her post-doctorate in special education technology at the University of Kentucky in 2006. She is the author or co-author of numerous refereed publications on the use of technology to improve students' learning. She has presented nationally and internationally on her research. She lives in Cincinnati with her husband Mike and son Bradley.

Alan Dichter is a former New York City teacher, principal, director of new school development, and a local instructional superintendent. He helped create and oversee New York's Executive Leadership Academy, a program designed to help leaders develop and incorporate facilitative leadership practices. He is the author of a number of articles on leadership and professional development and has consulted widely on issues related to urban school reform. He has also served as director of leadership development for the Portland, Oregon, public schools, and now does independent consulting. He is the co-author of *The Power of Protocols* and lives with his wife, Vivian, and sons, Ben and Jacob, in Portland.

Elizabeth C. McDonald is a master teacher in the Department of Teaching and Learning at the Steinhardt School of Culture, Education and Human Development at New York University. She co-leads NYU's introductory course in teacher education in which multiple sections each semester are all co-taught in New York City schools by NYC teachers. She also supervises elementary student teachers. She has been an elementary and middle-school teacher of students with special needs, a principal in both Massachusetts and New York, and a professional development specialist for the Rhode Island Department of Education. She is a co-author of *The Power of Protocols* and lives in New York City and Wareham, Massachusetts, with her husband, Joe, and their West Highland terrier.